School Library Media Centers
In
COOPERATIVE
AUTOMATION
PROJECTS

Compiled by Sally Drew and Kay Ihlenfeldt

for the

Multitype Library Networks and Cooperative Section,
Association of Specialized and Cooperatives Library Agencies,

and the

American Association of School Librarians

Divisions of the American Library Association, Chicago

ISBN 0-8389-7503-8

Printed in the United States of America

TABLE OF CONTENTS

INTRODUCTION

School library media centers throughout the country are planning or implementing automation programs involving single buildings or school districts. Increasingly, these programs are being carried out with other types of libraries on a local, regional, or statewide basis. There are few case studies of such cooperative programs documented in library literature, however. School library media center staff indicate that it is sometimes difficult to obtain information about, become involved in, or initiate planning for automation programs involving different types of libraries.

The American Library Association/Association of Specialized and Cooperative Library Agencies, Multitype Library Networks and Cooperatives Section (Multi-LINCS) and the American Association of School Librarians Publication Committees developed this publication about school library participation in cooperative automation projects in order to provide information about successful programs which are currently operational. Such programs often involve schools and other types of libraries or several school buildings which are geographically separated. An attempt has been made to include programs which have moved beyond the planning stage. Most have one or more functions fully operational and a few are in the implementation stage.

The programs described in these case studies and reports relate to the development of bibliographic databases (books, audiovisual materials, serials), sharing of online circulation systems or online catalogs, interlibrary loan telecommunication systems, production of microfiche or CD-ROM catalogs, and other automation activities.

This volume contains case studies which describe the administration of the program, the participating organizations, funding, goals, services and functions automated, equipment and software used, successes, problems, and future plans. In addition, short reports of many other automation programs are included. This is not intended to be an exhaustive list of programs, but is intended to illustrate the types of programs which are currently being carried out and which could be replicated in other places.

The table of contents shows the case studies and short reports organized by state and then by project name. The indices by project type and by type of automation system are included at the end of the publication.

ALABAMA

Alabama Union List of Serials

Administration: The program is now administered by the Alabama Public Library Service, the State Library Agency. It evolved into a statewide project from a joint project of the Pioneer Alabama Library System (PALS) and the Alabama Library Exchange (ALEX).

Participants: Twelve school libraries of all types and sizes are contributing members of the union list. The project is open to any Alabama library wishing to share resources through mail or walk-in service, and which agrees to contribute regular updates to its holdings.

The program currently includes approximately 115 academic, public, school, and special libraries. Most major state-supported colleges and universities, many of the public libraries, public library systems, and their member libraries are included. Some specialized and corporate libraries and schools at all levels individually or as a part of their local system collection also participate. Though any Alabama school library can participate, school members of ALEX were actively solicited and are the only ones which have elected to join.

Funding: The program has been funded with Library Services and Construction Act Title III funds since its inception in 1982. LSCA funds cover online maintenance of the database and production of the masters of the microfiche and paper editions. Until recently, LSCA paid for the cost of technical and project management staff, budgeted in FY90 at $38,000 with one half-time professional librarian for project coordination and one half-time paraprofessional for data entry. The staff is currently paid with state funds. Each participating library has received a microfiche copy of the current lists and a paper copy of its holdings at no cost. Libraries have the option of purchasing a paper copy of the entire list or a group subset at the cost of production. All database storage costs are born by the project.

Goals: The goals of the program at the onset were and continue to be:

Identification of the serials collections of libraries in the state.

Development of a bibliographic database to serve as a statewide resource sharing tool.

ALABAMA

Database Development: Originally produced in Phases I and II on a micro-computer as a title listing only, the project was the first SOLINET-based OCLC union list including enumeration and chronology; it later served as a model for several others. All updates and additions to the database, including the creation of new serials cataloging records at I or K level, are done at the project office. No decentralized data entry is currently being performed, as a quality control measure. Updating as changes occur is encouraged, but annual submissions of data are required.

Functions Automated: The primary intent was to create a location tool for identification of materials and to formulate a machine-readable database of bibliographic records. As with any OCLC union list, the holdings are immediately available online as changes are made and may be accessed by OCLC control number, ISSN, LC number, title, and corporate author.

Local libraries and groups of libraries have used subsets of the list in the creation of local automated programs including online catalogs, circulation systems, serials check-in files, and other local systems.

Several medical libraries have recently used their records extracted from the database in tape format to update their holdings in the National Library of Medicine's SERHOLD database for DOCLINE routing.

Description: In 1982, Phase I of the program included the identification of currently received titles in the collections and production of the list on the local microcomputer system. Phase II, beginning in 1984, involved the identification and addition of the retrospective holdings. Both Phases I and II were title listings only, while Phase III in 1985 began the first inclusion of specific enumeration of chronology as the holdings were first added to the Union Listings component of the OCLC Serials Control Subsystem, now called the Union Listing Subsystem.

Special Features: Libraries can extract their holdings from the database for loading into automated systems at the cost of tape production ($16.77 per tape in 1989) and a nominal cost per record. Groups of libraries may also request subsets of the list in paper format. Compiled at the time of the annual production, the group pays only the cost per page (about $.10) plus postage.

ALABAMA

Equipment Used: The original list was produced on a microcomputer, replaced by an OCLC 105 terminal. Initially, this terminal was the only equipment used, moving each time the project was relocated. In late 1989, this terminal was replaced by an OCLC M310 workstation. Project staff currently use OCLC M300 series workstations.

Interlibrary Loan or Delivery: Statewide distribution of the list in a variety of formats provides information of the serials holdings of a wide range of libraries representing all types and sizes. This affects interlibrary loan and walk-in access, allowing libraries to directly make requests for specific volumes and years, rather than having "blind" requests returned unfilled. Also, since records are chosen according to national union lists standards, libraries can use the list to verify the ISSN or OCLC number before making a request. Materials are delivered by mail or telefacsimile depending on the resources of the libraries involved and the speed in which they are needed.

Successes: The database now contains over 20,000 unique titles and in excess of 100,000 holdings statements, and was developed in accordance with national standards for union listing. Input standards and quality control criteria were implemented upon addition of on-site staff for management and supervision of the project, and an organized plan to clean up database discrepancies is progressing smoothly. Coordination of all processes involved in submitting holdings additions and changes, including centralized data entry, makes it simple for participating libraries to make timely and accurate updates. A standardized form for submissions and simple guidelines for reporting make it easy for library staff with varying levels of experience and expertise to keep holdings current. Over 65,000 annual uses of various records of AULS were estimated from a survey during the summer of 1989. Though no specific school library usage has been tracked, many are members of regional cooperatives which handle their ILL requests.

An editorial board consisting of librarians from around the state (both member and non-member) has been extremely useful in making recommendations for the union lists and giving guidance to the project staff. Representation from all types of libraries is included.

ALABAMA

Problems: In the early stages, the different levels of training and expertise of the input staff caused many technical and quality control problems, as did the fact that the technical and administrative staff were located in different cities. With the relocation of the project and its management and technical staff to the state library, these problems are expected to be solved.

A method to update by tapeload, currently being investigated by OCLC, would greatly enhance the ability to add larger collections with a minimum of title-by-title entry.

A problem generated by OCLC's inability to pull holdings by the 4-character "branch" symbol has created difficulties in billing for additional products.

Advice to Others: Emphasize from the beginning that libraries must be responsible for keeping their holdings current, to maintain an active, "living" database.

Hire staff to manage the program who are thoroughly familiar with union listing and serials standards; AACR2, revised ed.; MARC formats; and OCLC if planning to use.

Develop "user-friendly" training documentation for both project staff and library participants. Coordinate communication with library members, vendors, etc. through one administrative person to avoid confusion.

Appoint an advisory committee to assist in making policy revisions and recommendations to the project staff. Representation should include administrative, technical services and ILL personnel; familiarity with the library community and the political climate of all types of participating libraries should be a consideration in making appointments.

Future: Future plans include investigation of the possible inclusion of the union list of serials with the state library catalog on CD-ROM. An annual user's meeting during the state library convention and regular training workshops around the state are also planned.

ALABAMA

Contact Person: Cathy Clayton 205/277-7330 or Ruth Evans 205/277-7330.

Publications:

Alabama Union Lists of Serials (paper and microfiche editions). Copies may be purchased, subject to availability, by contacting the Alabama Public Library Service, 6030 Monticello Drive, Montgomery, AL 36130.

Birmingham Cooperative Circulation System

Contact person: Dr. Geraldine Bell
Address: Lane Teachers Center
410 13th Street South
Birmingham, AL 35233
Phone #:   205/583-4833

Project Description: Three high school libraries in the Birmingham City School System share use of the CLSI automated circulation system based at the Birmingham public Library with public libraries in Jefferson and Shelby Counties.

Participants: Check one

___ School buildings within a district
___ School libraries within a library cooperative or system
_x_ School library (ies) with public libraries
___ School library (ies) with other types of libraries
___ State level or statewide project
___ Other (specify)

Type of Project: Check all that apply

___ Development of bibliographic database(s)
___ Shared online catalog
_x_ Shared circulation system
___ CD-ROM, optical disk or microform catalogs
___ Interlibrary loan telecommunication systems
___ Other automated system

ALABAMA

LMN Cooperative Circulation System

Contact person: Charlotte Moncrief
Address: Library Management Network, Inc.
P.O. Box 443
Huntsville, AL 35804
Phone #: 205/532-5963

Project Description: Three high school libraries—two in Decatur and one in Hazel Green—share use of the Library Management Network (LMN) automated circulation system with junior college and public libraries across North Alabama. Other participants on the CLSI system include three junior colleges, four public library systems and one other public library. An online catalog is being developed. LMN is governed by a board representing its members.

Participants: Check one

___ School buildings within a district
___ School libraries within a library cooperative or system
___ School library (ies) with public libraries
_x_ School library (ies) with other types of libraries
___ State level or statewide project
___ Other (specify)

Type of Project: Check all that apply

___ Development of bibliographic database(s)
___ Shared online catalog
_x_ Shared circulation system
___ CD-ROM, optical disk or microform catalogs
___ Interlibrary loan telecommunication systems
___ Other automated system

ALASKA

Capital City Libraries

Administration: The Capital City Libraries (CCL) system is administered by the directors of the four participating libraries. Through a facilities maintenance contract the system is maintained by Library Systems of Alaska (LISA).

Participants: The original participants were the Alaska State Library and the Juneau Public Libraries. The Juneau Public Libraries includes three facilities: Juneau Public Library, Mendenhall Valley Public Library and Douglas Public Library. The University of Alaska Southeast joined the system in 1987. Juneau Douglas High School, the only high school in the Juneau School District, joined the other participants in July 1988.

Funding: Each participant has contributed to the central site equipment as follows: Alaska State Library $376,635 (68%); Juneau Public Libraries $153,850 (28%); University of Alaska Southeast Library $17,950 (3%); and Juneau Douglas High School Library $4,000 (.08%); total $522,435. Each library used local funds for staffing to link records and for on site equipment. Funding came from a variety of sources. The University of Alaska Southeast utilized interlibrary cooperation funds and general fund appropriations. Juneau Public Libraries monies came from CIP funds from new library construction. Juneau Douglas High School was able to join after obtaining monies from the Alaska State Library through an interlibrary cooperation grant for equipment, software licensing fees, a small contribution to central site equipment, and staff time to bar code materials. The Juneau School District matched those funds and added additional funds. A major effort was made by the other participants to include Juneau-Douglas High School in this project. Each library uses local funds based on an annual $1,000 per port charge for maintenance of the system.

Goals: The goals of Capital City Libraries are as follows:

To provide best possible library service to the citizens of Juneau of all ages through community-wide resource sharing.

To optimize limited resources through resource sharing and cooperative collection development.

ALASKA

To prepare students to become library and information literate.

To meet the needs for access to information in a state capital.

Development of an automated circulation system and online catalog which embodies the goals of community-wide resource sharing.

Development of a multi-type library system which uses one library card and provides direct loan to all patrons from member libraries.

Database development: Each member of CCL, with the exception of Juneau Douglas High School Library, was a member of the Western Library Network preceding the automation project. A tape was pulled from WLN for holdings of the three libraries and loaded into the Prime Computer as the CCL database. Additional tape loads from WLN have been done and an interactive download interface between LIS and WLN is now operational. Juneau Douglas High School does not belong to WLN and barcoded books as they were circulated. JDHS used a .5 staff person funded by the grant to bar code titles from the shelves. There are still several thousand local interim records which need to be converted to MARC records, the standard for the LIS database. The database now holds 327,692 items as follows: Juneau Public Libraries 36.17%; Juneau Douglas High School 3.46%; Alaska State Library and other state agencies 31.04%; University of Alaska Southeast Library 29.32%.

Functions Automated: Circulation, public access catalog, reserve room, technical services and community resource modules are currently operational; acquisitions, serials and CD server modules are under discussion.

Description: Planning for the project began in the early 1980s by the Alaska State Library. ASL was interested in a media booking system for the Alaska State Film Library. At the same time the WLN member libraries of Juneau began planning to produce a microfiche catalog of holdings of Juneau Libraries which was called the Capital CIty Libraries Catalog. The microfiche catalog was produced from 1984 to 1986. The automated system became operational in January of 1987 with the Alaska State Library and Juneau Public Libraries as participants using the circulation system and online catalog. The University of Alaska Southeast was also a participant and loaded its holdings in 1987 and began using the circulation system in 1988. Juneau Douglas High School joined in July, 1988. As part of the interlibrary cooperation grant each middle school (two) and elementary school (five) purchased a Link terminal. The staff at those libraries are using a limited number of dial-up ports to access information about resources outside their buildings. A library patron can search all six libraries' collections from any terminal, request material held, return materials to any library, and use any library directly with the Capital City Libraries Card.

Special Features: CCL system is a combined catalog of holdings of multitype libraries for the entire community, with direct loan to the public by all libraries and daily interlibrary courier delivery. Any person residing in Alaska may register for a free Capital City Libraries card. One special feature of the software is a display screen showing at a glance the holding of all libraries for each title. Systems policies are developed cooperatively by the directors and staff at the participating libraries and approved by the directors.

Equipment Used: For the Capital City Libraries' online system, LIS software is run on a Prime 9655 computer with eight megabytes of memory and three disc drives (two 315 megabyte drives and one 496 megabyte drive). The mainframe computer is locatd in the State Office Building in Juneau. Terminals at each location are customized Link terminals with a special function chip and customized key caps.

Interlibrary Loan or Delivery: Capital City Libraries uses a partially automated system for interlibrary loan. If the status for material wanted is "in" but at another library the patron must fill out a CCL loan card which is sent by courier to the owning library. Material is then sent by courier to the library where the patron wishes to pick up the material. If the material is "out" an electronic hold may be placed on the item and it is automatically sent via courier to the patron at the preferred library when the title is returned.

Successes: The entire community uses one library card. All libraries in the

ALASKA

community which belong to CCL are open to anyone. Books may be returned at any library. There are system wide policies which all libraries follow. Collection development is aided by cooperative collection. It is a multi-type resources sharing project whose concept is one library geographically dispersed. Each library can set its own borrowing parameters, so that a patron using the same library card has different borrowing privileges at different libraries. In a community of 30,000 there are currently 20,000 registered borrowers. With the same system in use in many libraries throughout the community we are able to provide library instruction to residents of all ages which is directly transferable. There is very little downtime on the system.

Problems: The Alaska State Library and the Juneau Public Libraries, the original participants, contracted with Library Information Systems to be a Beta test site. Being a Beta test site meant that Library Information Systems used the system for software development and in return CCL got customized software. There have been problems in bringing up a system in a developmental phase which have had to be dealt with. Don't underestimate the time and problems in staff morale and public relations that a system in flux brings. Everyone appreciates the customized software while complaints about the bugs. This is one way to bring up an automated system; and not necessarily the desired way unless you have very specialized needs. If you decide to "go this route" understand the problems that may occur. Setting of priorities for new items and items which do not yet work is set by a committee consisting of the directors of the four member libraries, representatives from public services and technical services from each library.

It has taken time to get to this committee structure which is used for priority setting for enhancements and for the order in which bugs will be fixed. Expectations grow - the more an automated system can do, the more people want it to do. Training and system documentation need to keep pace with development. These components, training and system documentation, need to be strong as they are a major factor in staff acceptance.

Advice to Others: Be innovative, be willing to try new things. Don't assume that schools in a community are not interested or can not participate in resource sharing. Be willing to sit down and talk as a group. Get everything in writing. Decide on the lines of communication for the decision making process beforehand.

Future: Capital City Libraries is about to complete the Beta test site phase and become completely operational. As with most library systems, we have already outgrown our Prime computer which no longer has the necessary computing power to meet the demands placed upon it. There are 90 ports operating on a system originally configured to handle 64 ports and response time is often below acceptable levels. Juneau Public Libraries has recently received permission from the City/Borough of Juneau to expend $200,000 from new library construction monies on a system upgrade. There is a $150,000 increment in the Alaska State Library budget for additional monies for the upgrade which requires legislative approval. A system upgrade is anticipated to cost $350,000. A system upgrade of the central site equipment will enable CCL to run faster and will allow more ports to be added at libraries throughout Juneau. Acquisitions, serials, and a more complete ILL system are planned. Planning for CD products to be accessed from any system terminal will be part of a system upgrade. Other specialized enhancements are being considered such as expansion of the community resource module and dial-up service to users.

Contact Persons: Karen Crane, State Librarian, Alaska State Library, P.O. Box G, Juneau, AK 99811, 907/465-2910. Donna Pierce, Director, Juneau Public Libraries, 292 Marine Way, Juneau, AK 99801, 907/586-5324. Michael Herbison, Director, University of Alaska Southeast Library, 11120 Glacier Highway, Juneau, AK 99801, 907/789-4467. Ann Symons, Juneau-Douglas High School Library, 10014 Crazy Horse Drive, Juneau, AK 99801, 907/586-2044.

Publications: None

ALASKA

Fairbanks North Star Borough School District CLSI Project

Contact person: Patricia Ann Thurman
Address: Fairbanks North Star Borough School District
Library Media Services Coordinator
Box 1250
Fairbanks, AK 99707-1250
Phone #: 907/456-7794

Project Description: Fairbanks North Star Borough Public Library and the Fairbanks North Star Borough School District's five high school library media centers share a CLSI system for circulation, and have a communal bibliographic database. Schools are being added to the online catalog as funding becomes available. As with all the libraries in Alaska, libraries are a part of the Alaska Library Network maintained through Western Library Network.

Participants: Check one

___ School buildings within a district
___ School libraries within a library cooperative or system
_x_ School library (ies) with public libraries
___ School library (ies) with other types of libraries
___ State level or statewide project
___ Other (specify)

Type of Project: Check all that apply

_x_ Development of bibliographic database(s)
_x_ Shared online catalog. Schools are being added as funds become available.
_x_ Shared circulation system
___ CD-ROM, optical disk or microform catalogs
___ Interlibrary loan telecommunication systems
___ Other automated system

First City Libraries Network

Contact person: Judy Arteaga
Address: Ketchikan High School
2610 Fourth Avenue
Ketchikan, AK 99901
Phone #: 907/225-9815

Project Description: The First City Libraries Network is an integrated automated area wide library system which is shared by city and borough offices, school libraries in the borough and the Ketchikan Public Library. When completed the system will include circulation, a public access catalog, acquisitions, serials, and an information and referral system.

Participants: Check one

___ School buildings within a district
___ School libraries within a library cooperative or system
_x_ School library (ies) with public libraries
___ School library (ies) with other types of libraries
___ State level or statewide project
___ Other (specify)

Type of Project: Check all that apply

___ Development of bibliographic database(s)
_x_ Shared online catalog
_x_ Shared circulation system
___ CD-ROM, optical disk or microform catalogs
_x_ Interlibrary loan telecommunication systems
_x_ Other automated system: serials

ALASKA

Sitka Library Network

Contact person: Harriet McClain
Address: Verstovia Elementary School
307 Kashevaroff Street
Sitka, AK 99835
Phone #:   907/747-8395

Project Description: Phase I of the project included entering all school district holdings, public library holdings, Sheldon Jackson College, Mt. Edgecumbe High School and several small agencies into the WLN database. A Shared Resources Catalog on microfilm was produced annually for three years.

Phase II of the project was to purchase a Library Information Services (LIS) automated system that includes online catalog, circulation and interlibrary loan features. The main computer is housed at the public library with terminals at seven locations in Sitka. Funding has been secured through the state legislature.

Participants: Check one

___ School buildings within a district
___ School libraries within a library cooperative or system
___ School library (ies) with public libraries
_x_ School library (ies) with other types of libraries: public, boarding school
___ State level or statewide project
___ Other (specify)

Type of Project: Check all that apply

_x_ Development of bibliographic database(s)
_x_ Shared online catalog
_x_ Shared circulation system
_x_ CD-ROM, optical disk or microform catalogs
_x_ Interlibrary loan telecommunication systems
___ Other automated system

CONNECTICUT

reQuest

Contact person: William Sullivan
Address: Connecticut State Library
231 Capitol Avenue
Hartford, CT 06106
Phone #: 203/566-2712

Project Description: ReQuest is a CD-ROM-based statewide database administered by the Connecticut State Library in collaboration with participating libraries through their representatives on the reQuest Executive Committee. Auto-Graphics is the vendor for the CD-ROM product which was built from data supplied by libraries using CLSI, Data-Phase, Geac, LS/2000 and OCLC source records. Each supplier worked independently with Auto-Graphics staff to ensure that tapes were readable. AMIGOS, by way of NELINET, extracted OCLC archive tapes for sending to Auto-Graphics. The goal is to include 1.4 million titles and 7.1 million holdings from more than 130 libraries, including schools, by August/September 1990. The immediate objective is to make the Catalog available to patrons at every principal public library, and every library whose holdings are in the Catalog, by June 30, 1991. This represents a total of approximately 218 libraries. Another objective is to update the Catalog three times annually. More than $2.2 million in funds will be expended by the Connecticut State Library to accomplish these objectives. Participating libraries are matching a portion of the cost. Reference: "From Amoeba to reQuest: a history and case study of Connecticut's CD-ROM-based statewide database," by William Uricchio & Michelle Duffy, pages 7-21 in Issue 30, Vol. 8, number 2 of Library Hi Tech.

Participants: Check one

___ School buildings within a district
___ School libraries within a library cooperative or system
___ School library (ies) with public libraries
___ School library (ies) with other types of libraries
_x_ State level or statewide project
___ Other (specify)

CONNECTICUT

Type of Project: Check all that apply

_x_ Development of bibliographic database(s)
___ Shared online catalog
___ Shared circulation system
_x_ CD-ROM, optical disk or microform catalogs
_x_ Interlibrary loan telecommunication systems
___ Other automated system

GEORGIA

Georgia Online Database (GOLD)

Contact person: JoEllen Ostendorf
Address: Georgia Division of Library Services
    156 Trinity Avenue, S.W., First Floor
    Atlanta, GA 30303-3692
Phone #:   404/656-2461

Project Description: GOLD is a group access capability through OCLC. School libraries and media centers are welcome to join. As of August 1990, three schools had joined. GOLD is used primarily for interlibrary loan and the union list of serials for Georgia.

Participants: Check one

___ School buildings within a district
___ School libraries within a library cooperative or system
___ School library (ies) with public libraries
___ School library (ies) with other types of libraries
_x_ State level or statewide project
___ Other (specify)

Type of Project: Check all that apply

_x_ Development of bibliographic database(s)
___ Shared online catalog
___ Shared circulation system
___ CD-ROM, optical disk or microform catalogs
_x_ Interlibrary loan telecommunication systems
_x_ Other automated system: union list of serials

IDAHO

VALNET

Contact person: Paul Krause, Director
Address: Lewis & Clark State College
8th Avenue and 6th Street
Lewiston, ID 83501
Phone #: 208/799-2227

Project Description: VALNET is an automation consortium including 18 academic, public and school libraries in the Lewiston, Idaho/Clarkston, Washington area. Lewiston city schools (elementary and secondary) are full participants in the CLSI system which includes database and circulation.

Participants: Check one

___ School buildings within a district
___ School libraries within a library cooperative or system
___ School library (ies) with public libraries
_x_ School library (ies) with other types of libraries
___ State level or statewide project
___ Other (specify)

Type of Project: Check all that apply

_x_ Development of bibliographic database(s)
_x_ Shared online catalog
_x_ Shared circulation system
___ CD-ROM, optical disk or microform catalogs
_x_ Interlibrary loan telecommunication systems
___ Other automated system

ILLINOIS

Cumberland Trail Library System Automation Services

Administration: Automated services provided to member libraries are administered by Cumberland Trial Library System (CTLS).

Participants: Cumberland Trail's automation project was established to create a shared database to facilitate resource sharing and to provide automated circulation control to participating libraries. All types of libraries are invited to participate. At present participating libraries include: two high school libraries, five academic libraries, and eight public libraries in addition to the system headquarter's library. All of these participants have entered their collections. Dial access to the database is available to other system member libraries. Participants must be members of the CTLS.

Funding: The automation project was established with LSCA funds in 1981. Ongoing costs for operation of the central computer facility has been absorbed by CTLS. Each participant purchases and maintains any equipment located in their library. The participating libraries also pay their own telecommunications charges. Members are billed for printing of overdue notices and reports. A new fee structure is being considered, as is a contribution from each member toward an automation development fund to cover the cost of expected upgrades. Staff costs are covered by CTLS headquarters.

Goals: The goals of CTLS were and continue to be:

Develop a union list of holdings to facilitate cooperative collection development and resource sharing.

Provide library automation services to CTLS members.

Database Development: CTLS purchased the database of the Johnson County Public Library, Shawnee Mission, KS on magnetic tape. This was loaded onto disk and member libraries matched against these records. If the item held by the member library was already in the database, they had to enter only their item information. If not, the bibliographic information was entered manually. The database has used the full MARC format from the beginning. An interface with the OCLC system is also used to add new holdings. The majority of the holdings of participating member libraries have been converted.

Functions Automated: The LS/2 software used by the CTLS Automation Project is a fully integrated system with the following functions available to users: circulation control, online catalog, public access catalog, public access catalog, mailbox, serials control, reports and notices, OCLC interface, and inventory.

Description: Project planning began in 1980 with implementation beginning in 1981. Data Phase ALIS II software was selected. OCLC and later Ameritech Information Systems purchased the ALIS II software which is now known as LS/2. The first libraries began using circulation control in March 1982. The project has added disk storage and upgraded the central processing unit (CPU) to accommodate additional libraries.

Special Features: All of the participating libraries are small (serving populations of less than 17,000) and are located in a rural area.

Equipment Used: Data General S/280 CPU and four Data General 190MB disk drives. Data General terminals are used along with some PCs with terminal emulation software. Dial-up libraries may access the database with most microcomputers. The software is the Data Phase ALIS II product now owned by Ameritech and renamed LS/2.

Interlibrary Loan or Delivery: The impact of the project has been most notable in interlibrary loan. With a shared database, libraries are borrowing more from each other, bypassing Cumberland Trail's interlibrary loan department. The shared database also makes it possible for more of the requests received by Cumberland's ILL department from non-participating libraries to be filled from within the library system. Cumberland's delivery service (van network) transports the bulk of these materials.

ILLINOIS

Successes: The database of approximately 500,000 items has become an important resource to all system member libraries. The electronic mail feature has helped to improve communication between participating libraries. Maintaining the operation and development of this automated system and planning for its future growth is in itself a significant achievement. The project has successfully demonstrated the value of library automation to small rural libraries.

Problems: Obtaining funding to make the necessary upgrades in both software and hardware is one of the principle problems encountered, as is the need to keep the cost within the reach of small libraries. The rising cost of telecommunications is also a problem. The time demands on central site staff is also a significant problem.

Advice to Others: Use only full MARC records in any automated system selected. Insist upon authority control from the start. In a library consortia all participants should be using LC subject headings. The quality of initial training and ongoing training is important for everyone using the automated system. It is also very important to provide adequate staff to operate the central site equipment. Long range planning for any project is also important.

Future: The process of issuing a request for information for replacement of both software and hardware is now underway. A detailed telecommunications study has been started. Efforts are also underway to secure the funding needed for the upgrade.

Contact person: Thomas J. (Joe) Harris, Head of Automation & Consulting Services, Cumberland Trail Library System, 12th & McCawley Streets, Flora, IL 62839, 618/662-2679.

Cumberland Trail Library System Automation Fact Sheet

Software: OCLC LS/2; originally Data Phase ALIS II. Data Phase sold all rights to the product to OCLC which renamed it LS/2 in December 1986. The computer system was first installed in January 1982. Automated functions include: circulation, PAC, cataloging, electronic mail, serials, etc.

Hardware: Data General S/280 CPU with 1MB memory and four Data General 190MB disk drives. The CPU currently has 48 ports or connections for terminals. OCLC recommends that no more than a total of 55 ports should be installed otherwise terminal users would experience a decline in response time. The computer system also has an operations console and line printer. Due to serious power supply problems which created an excessive amount of down time, a Liebert Datawave power conditioning system was installed in October 1987.

Participants: Participating libraries and number of terminals currently installed: (Note: each terminal requires one port on the computer)

Flora Carnegie Library	1
Fairfield Public Library	2
Frontier Community College	1
Fairfield High School	1
Wabash Valley College	3
Lincoln Trail College	2
Mt. Carmel Public Library	3
Centralia Public Library	4
Robinson Township Public Library	5
Rend Lake College	2
Salem High School	1
Evans Public Library, Vandalia	2
Olney Central College	1
C.E. Brehm Memorial Library, Mt. Vernon	4
Olney Carnegie Public Library	3
CTLS headquarters	8
Dial ports	2

Total Ports in Use	45

Telecommunications Equipment:

> 5 pair 8 channel multiplexers and 2400 baud modems
> 2 pair 4 channel multiplexers and 2400 baud modems
> 3 pair 1200 baud single line modems

Multiplexers are devices that permit several terminals to operate over one telephone line. Unless they are used, each remote terminal has to have its own telephone line. These units quickly pay for themselves by eliminating individual telephone lines. The following libraries are currently using multiplexers. The number following their name is the number of terminals currently in use.

> Olney Carnegie Library (3) and Olney Central College (1) via a 4 channel multiplexer

> Centralia Public Library (4) via 4 channel multiplexer

> Fairfield Public Library (2), Frontier Community College (1), and Fairfield High School (1) via an 8 channel multiplexer

> Evans Public Library, Vandalia (2) via an 8 channel multiplexer

> Wabash Valley College (3) and Mt. Carmel Public Library (3) via an 8 channel multiplexer

> Robinson Township Public Library (5) and Lincoln Trail College (2) via an 8 channel multiplexer

Cumberland Trail Library System Automation Department Staff:

The following CTLS staff members are assigned to manage the OCLC LS/2 computer system: Joe Harris, Head of Automation and Consulting Services; Becky Harrell, Automation Clerk; Nancy Williams, Order Department/Automation Clerk; and Evelyn Farmer, Cataloging/Automation Clerk. All have duties other than automation and spend varying amounts of time depending upon need. In order to provide adequate protection to the database a complete copy (this is also called a dump) of all data is made each weekday morning from 6:30 to 8:00 a.m. These staff members perform this duty on a rotating schedule. In addition they take turns serving in an on call capacity on weekends, holidays, and evenings when the system headquarters is closed. At least one automation department staff member is on duty at CTLS headquarters every weekday from 6:30 a.m. to 4:45 p.m., during the remainder of time the person on duty can be reached via a paging system.

Automation Cost Facts: The original installation of the computer system was financed in part by two LSCA Title I grants through the Illinois State Library. The cost of one terminal, OCR wand, and modems for each of the 14 libraries which went on line with CTLS in 1982 and 1983 was covered by these grants. Since the installation of the system in 1982 the CPU was upgraded from a Data General S/140 minicomputer with 256K memory and 32 ports installed to a Data General S/280 minicomputer with 1MB of memory and 48 ports installed with a capacity to support a total of 55. This upgrade was also partially financed by an LSCA grant.

In addition to the grant funding CTLS contributed a significant amount to cover installation costs such as remodeling a room to serve as the computer room, electrical wiring, air conditioning, considerable staff time, administrative and bookkeeping costs, and supplies which includes such items as disk packs, computer tape, and paper. Cumberland Trail headquarters also pays maintenance on the computer equipment located in its building, the software maintenance, and licensing fees.

Problems: OCLC has sold its Local Systems Division to Ameritech Information Systems. Prior to this sale OCLC notified all LS/2 users that it had stopped all development of its LS/Next software that was designed to provide a migration route for LS/2 users as well as LS/2000 users and that it would stop software support for LS/2 libraries effective January 1992. In addition to needing a system that would support additional terminals and an antiquated telecommunications network this presented a significant problem. Fortunately, plans have been made to remedy this situation.

Future: A detailed telecommunication study will be starting in the very near future with a goal of designing a more efficient and cost effective telecommunications network linking all of the present and possible future online libraries. Also plans have been made to investigate a replacement software and hardware system to replace the present OCLC LS/2 system.

How the sale of OCLC's Local Systems Division to Ameritech Information Systems will influence the development of the LS/2 software is unknown at this time. The goal over the next two years is to select a turnkey system that is capable of meeting the long term automation needs of Cumberland Trail's online libraries.

Bibliographic Records Summary
Cumberland Trail Library System
LS/2 System
6/5/89

System Library Name	PW #	Total Bib Count
Flora Carnegie	10	16,964
Bauer Media Center Wabash Valley College	14	15,310
Mt. Carmel Public	15	35,124
Rend Lake College	16	14,477
Media Center Salem Community High School	17	4,342
Learning Center Fairfield Community High School	18	7,426
Olney Carnegie Library	19	27,705
Learning Resource Center Lincoln Trail College	20	21,174
Cumberland Trail Library System	3	102,725
Learning Resource Center Frontier Community College & Olney Central College	4	12,408

Robinson Township District Public Library	5	33,460
Evans Public Library	6	20,267
C.E. Brehm Memorial Library	7	26,284
Fairfield Public Library	8	20,256
Centralia	9	41,876

Number of bib records used by more than one pw:	81,293
Total number of bib records in the system:	239,501
Total number of bib records with no items attached:	1,725
Total number of item records:	484,929

Contact Person: Thomas J. Harris, Head of Automation & Consulting Services, Cumberland Trail Library System, 12th & McCawley Streets, Flora, IL 62839, 618/662-2679.

Serials of Illinois Libraries Online (SILO)

Administration: The SILO program began at Northern Illinois University in 1982 as a Title III, Library Services and Construction Act Grant project to create a statewide union list of serials which would fully represent all Illinois regions. Due to the continued growth of the database and the increase in participating libraries, the SILO program has evolved from a grant project to a permanent program administered at the Illinois State Library, since July 1, 1987.

Participants: SILO membership is open to all Illinois academic, public, school, health science, law, and other special libraries of all sizes, clientele, and subject specialties.

The current membership in SILO includes over 750 multi-type libraries from all 18 Illinois library systems. Collections include 111 academic libraries, consisting of four-year colleges and universities, research and reference centers, community colleges, and theological seminaries; 229 public libraries; 168 school libraries; 123 health science libraries; 60 law libraries; and 67 other special libraries, including corporate, technical, and state agency libraries.

Funding: The SILO program has utilized Library Services and Construction Act funds since the program's inception in 1982. Ten library systems have received LSCA Title III grant funds to accommodate initial online costs associated with SILO participation, including OCLC profiling and data entry charges. Ongoing costs associated with SILO participation are paid by the member libraries. In addition, SILO activities funded by the Illinois State Library have included the purchase and distribution of periodic SILO Offline Products; labor costs for SILO updates for the holdings of selected non-OCLC SILO libraries; statewide training sessions offered; and production and distribution of SILO training materials and brochures.

Goals: The goals of the SILO program remain:

To create and maintain an accurate and comprehensive online union list of serials to include all types of libraries from all Illinois regions.

Illinois

To promote and expand bibliographic access and resource sharing capabilities.

To create automated linkages between SILO and the ILLINET Online database.

Database Development: The SILO program utilizes the OCLC Union List Subsystem to provide bibliographic data for verification and to report the copy-specific holdings of its member institutions. Over 350,000 holdings records from over 750 libraries comprise the SILO union list. Records are added to SILO in the following ways: 1) SILO members that are full OCLC members enter their own holdings; 2) Library systems that utilize SILO for all their union list activity perform the SILO data entry for their member libraries; and 3) The Illinois State Library creates and updates SILO records for non-aligned, non-OCLC SILO libraries. Holdings are formatted in accordance with the ANSI Standard on Serial Holdings Statements at the Summary Level.

Functions Automated: The intent of the SILO program was to replace the multiplicity of labor intensive, hard copy union lists with one consolidated online statewide list, in order to enhance bibliographic access and ensure a greater efficiency, accuracy, and currency of reported holdings. Online access is supplemented with the availability of OCLC Offline Products on paper, microfiche, and magnetic tape.

Description: In 1979, a Union List Subcommittee of the Illinois OCLC Steering Committee was established to analyze the feasibility of a statewide online union list of serials in Illinois. Various bibliographic databases were investigated, including LCS, CLSI, OCLC, and several other commercial vendors. The Union List Component of OCLC was the top ranking contender of all the systems examined.

The efforts of the Union List Subcommittee study ultimately led to the submission of a grant proposal to the Illinois State Library Advisory Committee, seeking funding for the SILO Union List Project. In September 1981, Northern Illinois University was awarded a $145,000 LSCA Title III grant to create the foundation for a statewide, online serials union list, using the OCLC Union List Component.

ILLINOIS

A central serials union list office was established at Northern Illinois University to coordinate the project, select and train staff from participating libraries, and begin a database of serials holdings that would include all types of libraries, representing all Illinois regions.

By the end of June 1983, 77 libraries had entered their serials holdings into the SILO Union List. These libraries included 24 academic, 18 public, five school, and 30 special libraries, contributing over 80,000 serials holdings.

The continuation of the SILO project was funded with LSCA Title III grant funds for two additional phases of the project. By the end of SILO Phase 3, June 1986, SILO membership had more than quadrupled, going from 77 to 329 member libraries, with a database that had nearly tripled, containing over 200,000 serials holdings.

The continued growth of the database and member libraries allowed for SILO's evolution from a grant funded project to a permanent program at the Illinois State Library, effective July 1987. The scope of holdings and the number of member libraries continue to increase in SILO. With a current membership of over 750 libraries, SILO ranks as the third largest of 100 OCLC Union List groups.

Special Features: The use of OCLC for SILO Union List activity provides the following benefits:

1. Efficiency. System-supplied bibliographic data allows for keystroking to be limited to local holdings information only. Also, libraries can belong to more than one union list group in OCLC without requiring additional data entry or incurring multiple storage fees.

2. Currency. Holdings information can be updated as often as desired, thus, maximizing the probability of accurate holdings statements.

3. Open membership. OCLC allows non-OCLC libraries to report their holdings in the Union List Subsystem, thus, establishing a broad base for serials resource sharing and extending statewide access to the many unique serials collections of small special libraries.

4. Inclusion of non-serials materials in SILO. Since July 1990, OCLC has extended the use of the Union List records to include materials from all

bibliographic formats. SILO members, are therefore, encouraged to create supplemental SILO lists for varying types of materials (e.g. sound recordings, videotapes, maps, etc.) This extended service should result in an improved capability for resource sharing and access to new collections, particularly from non-OCLC SILO libraries.

5. Offline products. Union list records, in addition to being accessible in the OCLC online system, are also available two times yearly through OCLC produced offline products on paper, microfiche, and magnetic tape.

6. Access to the OCLC Interlibrary Loan Subsystem for non-OCLC SILO libraries. Through OCLC's Group Access Capability, non-OCLC SILO members can become "selective users," whereby they subscribe to the ILL Subsystem only. As selective users, non-OCLC SILO libraries can perform online interlibrary loan transactions, access the entire OCLC Online Union Catalog, and view all Illinois holdings on OCLC. Furthermore, requests that cannot be filled within the state can be referred out of state through the Illinois State Library.

Equipment Used: Libraries using terminal software can use the OCLC M300, M310, M386, M220, or any IBM compatible computer for SILO data entry. OCLC dial-access users that do not use the OCLC software can access the OCLC Union List Subsystem using any computer with communications capabilities (e.g. third party communications software, such as Smartcom, Crosstalk, Procom, etc.).

Interlibrary Loan or Delivery: The SILO program has strengthened resource sharing, both statewide and nationwide, by providing access to over 750 Illinois serials collections. Additionally, SILO records provide the only detailed copy-specific holdings on OCLC for Illinois libraries, thus, increasing interlibrary loan efficiency. Furthermore, the selective user option for non-OCLC SILO members has increased the overall volume of interlibrary loan transactions on OCLC for Illinois libraries.

Successes: Currently, the SILO Union List Program is the third largest of 100 OCLC Union List groups, with over 750 participating libraries contributing over 350,000 holdings. Support for SILO has been strong among all types of libraries in all Illinois regions.

In addition to OCLC access, many health science SILO libraries benefit from SILO by loading their SILO records in SERHOLD, NLM's database of machine-readable holdings statements for serial titles, containing approximately 1,035,000 holdings statements for about 34,000 serials titles from over 2,400 health science libraries nationwide. With their holdings in SERHOLD, these health science SILO libraries can perform online ILL transactions utilizing DOCLINE, NLM's interlibrary loan request and referral system. Essentially, as SILO members, these libraries can update DOCLINE easily and cheaply.

Finally, the selective user option has enabled many smaller libraries online access to OCLC. Those benefiting include libraries whose limited cataloging needs, coupled with budget constraints would otherwise make OCLC use unfeasible.

Problems: Quality control remains an ongoing challenge for the SILO program. The need to ensure that SILO records remain current and accurate is a primary concern of the Illinois State Library.

An important function of the SILO program is the monitoring of union list activity, via OCLC usage reports, to ensure that member libraries update the holdings regularly. To further ensure the currency of the database, the Illinois State Library regularly updates the holdings of all non-OCLC SILO participants, whose library systems, consortia, etc., are unable to provide that service. Also, ILLINIT/OCLC libraries are encouraged to report any incorrect or substandard SILO holdings records to the Illinois State Library for corrections.

Advice to Others: 1) To achieve the maximum accuracy and quality of a large union list, it is important to pursue the participation of special interest subgroups, rather than just individual libraries. In SILO, these subgroups consist of 10 Illinois library systems; Health Science Librarians of Illinois (HSLI); Chicago Association of Law Libraries (CALL); Chicago Area of Theological Libraries Association (CATLA); SILO Service Center of the Chicago Library System; Northern Illinois Learning Resources Centers (NILRC); Southern Illinois Learning Resources Centers (SILRC); and the SeCo Fax Consortium, a group of school libraries in southern Illinois. These groups utilize SILO for all their union list activity, and thus, have a vested interest in keeping their SILO records updated.

2) Provide clear and detailed training materials and workshops for new member libraries. In addition to training the data entry staff, there should also be workshops for reference and interlibrary loan staff to ensure maximum use of the database. Furthermore, promotional materials should always stress the link between union listing and the resulting increase in interlibrary loan capability.

Future: Future plans include: 1) the creation of automated linkages between SILO and the ILLINET Online database; 2) the loading of SILO holdings into the CARL UnCover database for accessing contents notes from over 10,000 serials titles. The SILO Carl UnCover records will be accessible through a telecommunications link through ILLINET Online; and 3) the inclusion of a greater scope of holdings in SILO that reflects all bibliographic formats.

Contact Person: Suzanne Schriar, Illinois State Library, Illinet/OCLC Services, 300 South Second Street, Room 410, Springfield, IL 62701-1796, 217/785-1532.

Publications:

Serials of Illinois Libraries Online Handbook. Springfield, IL: Illinois State Library, 1988, editor.

Schriar, Suzanne. "Results of the SILO Survey in Illinois," Illinois Libraries, December 1987, pp. 698-700.

Schriar, Suzanne. "The Future of SILO at the Illinois State Library," Illinois Libraries, December 1987, pp. 700-701.

Schriar, Suzanne. "SILO: The Evolution of the Serials of Illinois Libraries Online Union List Program," Illinois Libraries, January 1989, pp. 54-56.

SILO brochure, January 1990.

SILO Terminal Guide, January 1990.

OCLC LS/2 Automation System

Contact person: Deborah S. Rodgers
Address: Shawnee Library System
Greenbriar Road
Carterville, IL 62918
Phone #: 618/985-3711

Project Description: Shawnee Library System, a multi-type library system/organization, has an online bibliographic database comprised of the collections of one system library, three public libraries, and one academic library. Libraries share the same bibliographic record, but the computer software allows each library to have autonomous circulation and online catalog systems.
The online catalog does allow the user to view the holdings of all five libraries. Currently, five school libraries have either dial access or dedicated line access to the online public access catalog. The schools also use the electronic mail function to send their interlibrary loan requests to the system library.

Participants: Check one

___ School buildings within a district
_x_ School libraries within a library cooperative or system
___ School library (ies) with public libraries
___ School library (ies) with other types of libraries
___ State level or statewide project
___ Other (specify)

Type of Project: Check all that apply

_x_ Development of bibliographic database(s)
_x_ Shared online catalog
_x_ Shared circulation system
___ CD-ROM, optical disk or microform catalogs
_x_ Interlibrary loan telecommunication systems
_x_ Other automated system: dial access

ILLINOIS

Project INFORM

Contact person: Eva R. Brown
Address: Director, Multi-type Library System Development
    Chicago Library System
    1224 W. Van Buren Street, Suite 634
    Chicago, IL 60607
Phone #:   312/738-7694

Project Description: A pilot project links public high school libraries with the Chicago Public Library, providing online access to the CPL collections. Currently, six high school libraries of the Chicago Public Schools access the CPL online catalog, with potential for reciprocal access. Planning is also underway to extend the project to all 69 high school libraries.

Participants: Check one

___ School buildings within a district
___ School libraries within a library cooperative or system
_x_ School library (ies) with public libraries
___ School library (ies) with other types of libraries
___ State level or statewide project
___ Other (specify)

Type of Project: Check all that apply

___ Development of bibliographic database(s)
_x_ Shared online catalog
___ Shared circulation system
___ CD-ROM, optical disk or microform catalogs
___ Interlibrary loan telecommunication systems
___ Other automated system

Rolling Prairie Library System CLSI Network

Contact person: Paul V. Johnson
Address: Rolling Prairie Library System
    345 W. Eldorado Street
    Decatur, IL 62522
Phone #:   217/429-2586

Project Description: Rolling Prairie Library System, a multi-type library system/organization, has an automated resource sharing network of 19 central Illinois libraries. The shared database of 400,000 items and 210,000 titles is housed on a CLSI Altos computer located at the system headquarters. Membership is currently 15 public libraries, two academic libraries, two school libraries and the system headquarters.

Participants: Check one

___ School buildings within a district
_x_ School libraries within a library cooperative or system
___ School library (ies) with public libraries
___ School library (ies) with other types of libraries: public, academic
___ State level or statewide project
___ Other (specify)

Type of Project: Check all that apply

_x_ Development of bibliographic database(s)
_x_ Shared online catalog
_x_ Shared circulation system
___ CD-ROM, optical disk or microform catalogs
_x_ Interlibrary loan telecommunication systems
___ Other automated system

Starved Rock Library System CLSI Network

Contact person: Richard Wilson
Address: Starved Rock Library System
900 Hitt Street
Ottawa, IL 61350
Phone #: 815/434-7537

Project Description: The Starved Rock Library System has a CLSI based union catalog. All schools (elementary and high school) contribute cards and system staff tag the record in the database. Library staff have dial access to check the holdings. Schools may contract for dial access to the database which has been created by the system.

Participants: Check one

___ School buildings within a district
_x_ School libraries within a library cooperative or system
___ School library (ies) with public libraries
___ School library (ies) with other types of libraries
___ State level or statewide project
___ Other (specify)

Type of Project: Check all that apply

_x_ Development of bibliographic database(s)
___ Shared online catalog
_x_ Shared circulation system
___ CD-ROM, optical disk or microform catalogs
_x_ Interlibrary loan telecommunication systems
_x_ Other automated system: dial access

SWAN (System Wide Automated Network)

Contact person: Lois Schultz
Address: Suburban Library System
                        125 Tower Drive
                        Burr Ridge, IL 60521
Phone #:   708/325-6640

Project Description: School libraries may participate in the Suburban
Library System's shared automated CLSI circulation system which provides
access to 850,000 titles in participating libraries. One high school (Reavis
High School, Burbank) participates in this automated network. Others may
use dial access.

Participants: Check one

___ School buildings within a district
_x_ School libraries within a library cooperative or system
___ School library (ies) with public libraries
___ School library (ies) with other types of libraries
___ State level or statewide project
___ Other (specify)

Type of Project: Check all that apply

___ Development of bibliographic database(s)
_x_ Shared online catalog
_x_ Shared circulation system
___ CD-ROM, optical disk or microform catalogs
_x_ Interlibrary loan telecommunication systems
_x_ Other automated system: dial access

INDIANA

Carmel's Public Library/School Libraries Shared Integrated Online System

Administration: The Carmel Clay Public Library and Carmel Clay Public Schools Shared Computer Project is administered by a Joint Board of four persons — two appointed by the Public Library Board of Trustees and two by the schools' director of media services and the systems coordinator (who is also the library's head of technical services) serve on the Joint Board in an ex-officio capacity. The Joint Board meets semi-annually to approve policy for operation of the system and to adopt a budget with the consent of their respective boards.

An Advisory Committee recommends to the Joint Board the budget for operating the system, recommends policies, establishes procedures, and maintains standards of operation. The committee is comprised of the library's director, technical services librarian/system coordinator, computer operator, and a public services librarian as well as the school's director of media services, cataloger, and two media specialists. Other staff members from both agencies are invited to attend any time and provide input.

Participants: When the project is completed in 1991, every resident of Clay Township (pop. est. 43,289) will have access to all public library and school library collections through intrasystem loans and/or walk-in loans. Total number of libraries and students are: one public library, one high school with 1,854 students, two junior highs (grade 6-9) with 2,454 students, and seven elementary schools with 3,798 students.

Funding: All central site costs, including hardware and software, are shared equally. In this project neither agency is contracting from the other. It is a totally shared system. Libraries have used local funds for staffing to carry out retrospective conversion, update the database, and for equipment.

The schools used ECIA-2 money for some equipment, their cumulative building fund, capital projects fund, a holding corporation/construction fund, and their general fund. The public library used construction funds from a bond issue and their general operating fund. An LSCA grant was used to hire an independent researcher/consultant to evaluate the project. All bills of a joint nature are paid by the library with the school reimbursing for their share.

Goals: The original goals continue to be: Provide better access to the collections, improve user services, permit more efficient library service, and promote resource sharing and cooperation between the libraries in Clay Township.

Database Development: Contributors to the database agreed from the beginning to use full MARC records. The public library started with 27% of their records already on OCLC. Retrospective conversion was completed using MICROCON (a retrospective conversion service from OCLC) and cataloging online with OCLC. The schools check their records against the local database. The records for which there is no local match are cataloged online with OCLC.

Both agencies utilized OCLC RETROCON for established collections and the standard pricing structure for current cataloging. A local MARC record was created for fewer than 1% of the items in the database. Each agency is responsible for cataloging and updating their records in both the local and OCLC databases.

Functions Automated: A main concern was to create a single machine-readable database of bibliographic records and holdings to assist library staff, community patrons, students and faculty in identifying the location of materials. In addition, patron records from the library and the schools are integrated.

Currently in use are public access online terminals; circulation control including overdues, inventory, circulation statistics, and reserves. An electronic bulletin board is available but seldom used because it is easier to pick up the phone and get an immediate response. The agencies are all in the same area so there are no long distance charges involved. An acquisitions module is available but staffing limitations prevent its use at this time. Serials control is available also, but economically impractical for a system our size.

Cataloging is done on OCLC workstations at the public library and at the school's Office of Media Services. The bibliographic records are downloaded to the local CLSI system via interfaces.

INDIANA

Description: Initial exploration for the project began in 1984. In 1985 the request for proposal was written, accepted and the CLSI contract signed in November. The project was implemented in conjunction with construction and remodeling of the public library and a school referendum.

The public library had been using OCLC since 1982. Retrospective conversion began in the fall of 1985; circulation began online in April 1987; followed by use of public access terminals in March 1988.

The schools began conversion of one elementary school and the high school in 1986, matching against the public library database. The elementary school was circulating online and had public access computers available in 1987, with the high school following the next spring. Conversion of the two junior high schools was completed in 1989 and a new elementary school opened in 1989 with online public access catalogs only (no card catalog). All retrospective conversion is expected to be completed by December 1990 for the five remaining elementary schools and the school's Educational Services Center is projected to be fully functioning in 1991.

Special Features: The RFP was written in three ways since it was a time of transition and decision-making because of the tentative nature of school funding. The Interlocal Cooperation Agreement was written pursuant to IC 36-1-7-1 et seq., having to do with the same geographical area.

Overdue notices and circulation statistics can be generated at both the central site and at individual remote sites from information compiled at the central site using the integrated patron database. All sites issue the same plastic, credit card type borrower's cards, which can be used at any location in the system. The school courier makes daily stops at each agency.

Equipment Used: The central site equipment consists of DEC PDP hardware with CLSI's proprietary operating system. In 1990 Altos hardware will be installed with a UNIX operating system. Most terminals are Wyse brand. The schools each have at least two Facit printers for circulation and online catalog. Laser bar code readers are CC80 and CC90. Two Apple computers have been modified for MARC edit and circulation soft backup use.

Interlibrary Loan or Delivery: Forms (3x5) for intrasystem loans were developed to record patron requests. The requests are placed by phone, and materials are delivered daily by school courier. Articles may be sent via FAX. So far the public library borrows more items from the schools than vice versa because of the longer library hours, the schools being closed in the summer, and not all schools online yet.

Successes: The Advisory Committee and the Joint Board concepts working in conjunction with the Interlocal Cooperation Agreement, have allowed the project to work very smoothly and successfuly. A complete database of materials is available to the entire community. These items are successfully loaned by the intrasystem loan procedures utilizing a daily delivery system.

Policies and procedures continue to be amicably developed. The Advisory Committee has met monthly for almost three years and has never had to vote on an issue, preferring to work toward consensus instead.

In addition to the Advisory Committee, the cooperative relationship between the library and the schools continues to thrive. Public library staff are invited to participate in school media meetings. Media specialists and teachers use assignment alert forms developed by the public librarians who also developed a notification letter they sign to verify when a student has tried unsuccessfully to locate resources at the public library. The schools actively promote the library Summer Reading Program by printing and distributing information about it.

Sharing Carmel's experiences with the library profession through speeches, articles, and conference presentations has been positive. Other successes include the LSCA Evaluation Report, the positive community perception and the recognition within the library community. The Shared Computer System was instrumental in the Carmel Clay Public Library being presented with the 1990 Indiana Outstanding Library of the Year Award.

Problems: The decision made at the onset to use a common patron bar code numbering system makes distinction of fines between library and school patrons awkward. Overdue notices are a problem. Converting from a manual system that works fine to an automated system where compromises had to be made required patience and a spirit of good will since the two methods cannot be overlaid. The library notices were designed for U.S.

mail, not for school homeroom use. Not all automation processes smoothly replace manual operations.

The issue of bibliographic control requires more cataloging staff time because of cooperative decision-making and spot checking for bibliographic record integrity. Automation also requires a higher level of staff expertise and knowledge in order to adhere to the bibliographic standards commitment. We have found additional cataloging help and a computer operator's time are required. It also takes additional time to write joint policies, procedures, and training manuals; to train new staff; and in technical services, to withdraw lost and paid items which must be deleted locally then on OCLC. Because we were a test site with no model to follow, developing procedures has been time consuming.

The school's closing for the summer and in the evenings somewhat restricts public library use. The high school has extended its hours one afternoon a week and two of the elementary schools have opened a couple of hours one evening a week. In the summer, courier service is cut back to three times a week.

Present inventory procedures on the automated system are difficult and take more time. The schools would like to do an annual inventory which is cumbersome because books have to be taken individually from shelves and have the bar codes scanned.

Reliance on telecommunications is a concern whether it is trouble with leased phone lines, the system going down or circulation problems. Expenses are on-going. New equipment and software are developed regularly. The decision to join OCLC was expensive, and as yet there is no inexpensive serials control module available. An automation system creates great expectations which cannot always be accommodated — whether because of cost, space, or time.

Advice to Others: Include only full MARC records in the database. Talk to other librarians who have similar systems and find out the problems and pitfalls.

Establish procedures for carefully documenting hardware and software difficulties, including a method of tracking equipment sent for repairs. A log showing a pattern of breakdown assists the vendor in trouble shooting. Designate a key trouble shooter. Develop a clear, concise procedures manual.

Recognize that an automated system will not save money, but it does provide a tremendous community service. Realize that even with a shared system there is a need for some duplication of materials. Institute a continous public relations program to remind taxpayers of the value they are getting for their dollars.

In planning a budget, allow adequate funds for additional staff and for them to attend Users Group meetings and training sessions.

Future: We plan to continue our existing services and add enhancements such as acquisitions, materials booking, serials control, dial access allowing patrons to use the system at home, etc., as they are developed and funds allow.

We need to resolve library and school closing schedules for summer, weekends, and holidays.

Development of a circulation procedures manual will be completed. And we would like to acquire portable terminals for inventory control in the schools, and explore adding area private schools to the system.

Contact Persons: Wendy A. Phillips, System Coordinator, Carmel Clay Public Library, 515 East Main Street, Carmel, IN 46032, 317/844-6255. Karen K. Niemeyer, Director of Media Services, Carmel Clay Schools, 5201 East 131st Street, Carmel, IN 46032, 317/844-9961. Patricia J. Allen, Director, Carmel Clay Public Library, 515 East Main Street, Carmel, IN 46032, 317/844-6711.

Publications:
Access (Carmel Clay Schools), 1, No. 1 (February 1987) and 2, No.3 (May 1980).

Hooten, Patricia A. Carmel's Shared System: A Report. September 30, 1988.

INDIANA

Hooten, Patricia A. "Online Catalogs: Will They Improve Children's Access?" Youth Services in Libraries. Spring 1989, pp. 267-272.

Niemeyer, Karen K. "Commitment, Cooperation and Compromise: Shared Online Computer System," Media Spectrum. Fourth Quarter 1988, pp. 28-30.

Nytes, M. Jacqueline "Networking Close to Home: A Shared On-Line Computer System," Indiana Libraries, 7 No. 1 (1988), pp. 15-20.

Nytes, M. Jacqueline, Wendy Phillips, Karen Opal, et al. A Request for Proposals for the Purchase, Installation, and Maintenance of an Integrated Online Library System at the Carmel Public Library. Issued May 31, 1985.

Local newspaper series and workshop presentation packet.

Forthcoming:
Hooten, Patricia A. Perspectives in Library Automation. ALA 1990.

Niemeyer, Karen K. "Library Management Systems: What Will They Do for Students?" School Library Media Quarterly, Summer 1990.

Iowa

Iowa Locator

Contact person: Dan Cates
Address: State Library of Iowa
East 12th and Grand
Des Moines, IA 50319
Phone #:   515/281-4499

Project Description: Sponsored by the State Library of Iowa, the Iowa Locator is a bibliographic database containing the holdings of over 500 multi-type libraries in the state of Iowa. More than five million holdings of over one million books are transcribed on three CD-ROM discs. This information is accessible through the 140 microcomputer-based Iowa Locator stations, five of which are in Iowa school libraries. Items found on the Iowa Locator can then be requested on the Iowa Computer Assisted Network thus facilitating prompt delivery of needed items. Libraries which contribute their holdings to the Locator may also purchase their MARC records at a very reasonable price for cooperative activities at the local level. Records and holdings of all libraries in the state are actively solicited for the Iowa Locator database.

Participants: Check one

____ School buildings within a district
____ School libraries within a library cooperative or system
____ School library (ies) with public libraries
____ School library (ies) with other types of libraries
_x_ State level or statewide project
____ Other (specify)

Type of Project: Check all that apply

_x_ Development of bibliographic database(s)
____ Shared online catalog
____ Shared circulation system
_x_ CD-ROM, optical disk or microform catalogs
_x_ Interlibrary loan telecommunication systems
____ Other automated system

MINNESOTA

North Country Library Cooperative Multi-type Database Activities

Administration: North Country Library Cooperative (NCLC) is one of seven multi-county, multi-type library networks in the state of Minnesota. The multi-type is regulated by state law and is considered part of the state department of education. The office of Library Development and Service (LDS) administers the grant applications process for state and LSCA title III monies. The cooperative has a 23 member citizens Governing Board and a professional librarians Advisory Committee. The board employs a full-time director to administer the program.

Participants: NCLC was established for the purpose of encouraging all types of libraries to work together. There are currently 10 academic libraries, 29 public libraries (this includes one public library system with bookmobile and mail-a-book service), 112 school libraries/media centers, and 17 special libraries.

Special efforts are made to include school and special libraries because by nature and through geographic placement they tend to be more isolated than either academic or public libraries. NCLC encompasses 18,000 square miles, most of which is sparsely populated. The last available census figures show a population of 320,000 for this region. It is assumed that the 1990 census will show a marked decrease due to an unfavorable economic climate in the region which occurred in the early to mid 1980s related to the mining and shipping industries.

School libraries constitute the largest portion of our membership and we have the majority of those members participate in projects such as the union serials list and other resource sharing activities. Funding at the individual institutional level still prevents many school libraries from participating in MARC conversion through LaserQuest. Also, participation in the regional electronic mail and bulletin board will be limited at the institutional level depending on what equipment is available from school district to school district.

Funding: The Minnesota cooperatives are funded by both state and LSCA Title III funds since their inception in 1979. NCLC has an operating budget of $82,874. Approximately 55% is LSCA money and 45% state funding. Additional grants are solicited from independent agencies for special projects. Membership fees are not charged to participating libraries. The MARC conversion process participants are assessed a per record fee of $.20 to defray the cost of additional personnel.

Goals: The overall goal of the cooperative is improving library and information services by developing programs which lead to sharing human and material resources as well as improving levels of expertise. The communication component is essential because not only does it foster professional fellowship, it also permeates the feeling of isolation often felt in rural areas. Partnerships become easier to forge between various types of libraries — most notably school and public libraries — for lifelong learning skills.

Database Development: General Research Corporation's LaserQuest is used to convert member records to MARC format. We utilize their database maintenance program so records are loaded in for storage and future implementation of a regional CD-ROM union catalog. The individual library is given a MARC tape to use in whatever system they have selected for their institution.

The regional union serials list was also compiled by matching records on LaserQuest. The company prepared a union profile which enabled us to call up the periodical record and add the individual institution holdings of a particular periodical. Deletions are done the same way. A microfiche union serials list was produced because many libraries (particularly elementary and middle schools) do not have access to computers in their libraries.

Not all libraries agree that MARC format is necessary, or completely understand the need for a standard. By assuming control of record conversion we are assuring the region of having records that are standardized. Libraries are free to select and use any in-house system they wish.

Currently the fiche product suits everyone's immediate need. When the database is large enough the MARC formatted union serials list will be merged with book and AV holdings in a CD-ROM product.

Each library is assured that its cataloging will remain intact. Local notes and local subject heads will be retained, however, NCLC selects the MARC record the local information is attached to so as to insure complete cataloging. All entries and deletions are handled by NCLC staff to assure some semblance of uniformity.

Functions Automated: Machine readable records for all holdings are being created, and electronic network is in the development process, and cooperative members are able to more readily identify what each other owns.

The electronic network will be an easy to use, toll-free means to tap into regional library news, send correspondence, ask for reference assistance, transmit ILL requests and conference.

The host system will have multiple dial in ports so at least three libraries can be accommodated at the same time. Screen design of the ILL module is the same as the paper request forms members have used for the past two years. A database tracking feature will be built into the system to enable NCLC to produce statistical reports as an aid in collection development and assure copyright compliance. The electronic network will be accessible by either IBM (or clone) or Apple Computers.

Description: Planning for database development has been an ongoing project since the inception of the multi-type cooperatives in Minnesota (1979). During that time period enthusiasm has waxed and waned according to projected fund levels. Two separate studies were done during the eight year period by outside consultants to determine feasibility of developing a shared system. Costs were determined to be prohibitive. A shift in focus from a shared system concept to independent automation efforts emerged in the later 1980's. In 1989 the cooperative began record conversion and database building. In March of 1990 the first union serials list was distributed to members and planning began on the electronic network which is slated to be operable in September of 1990.

Equipment Used: An Epson Equity II computer with 5 Daisy chained Hitachi CD ROM reader is used for record conversion using the LaserQuest system. The same system is used for the union serials list.

For the electronic network a dedicated computer will be used with an 80MB hard disc, 60 MHz 386 processor, multi-modem and 2MB RAM. The NCLC director is working with a programmer to design a menu driven communication network based on three letter codes assigned to each member library. Desqview/386 by Quarterdeck will be used with a database interface.

Interlibrary Loan or Delivery: Once the union serials list was delivered, the libraries were able to readily locate material and borrow from each other directly. North Country Library Cooperative and the regional public library system (Arrowhead Library System) pay associated costs to maintain a Reference and Referral Center which processes ILL requests, answers reference requests and prepares online literature searches. Associated costs of maintaining this service should measurably decrease with the capability of identifying the location of needed material. The speed of information delivery is also improved because of the ability to directly request material. Also, the cooperative initiated a courier system which will service 16 cities on a daily basis. Initial start-up costs were obtained through a grant and subsequent costs will be co-shared between the Arrowhead Library System, MINITEX, Arrowhead Community College System and the Arrowhead University Center.

Successes: Everything completed to date has greatly improved the ability to share resources and communicate between the regional libraries. We are winning the battle to eliminate barriers to access across all types of libraries and better managing the vast land distances between libraries. The overall response from libraries has been very positive. School librarians in particular have noted that they feel less isolated and appreciated the fact that they are able to fill requests for their students more rapidly.

Problems: Money is the major obstacle to overcome. Our time line is directly related to availability of cash. Regional librarians have been outstanding in contributing serial holdings in a timely manner as well as embracing the concept of direct borrowing.

Many problems were avoided by NCLC staff compiling the data entry. We felt that it was important that libraries retain their own identity during record conversion. The approach taken was not that their cataloging was incorrect, but that we were able to enhance their records during the conversion process.

How, when, and if ILL requests are filled continues to be somewhat of a problem but that always will be the case when you work with 184 separate personalities and policies. Abandoning the concept of a shared system eliminated most problems before they had the opportunity to surface.

Advice to Others: Approach any plan with a holistic view and a clear understanding of bottom line needs. Listen intently to what members want to accomplish and throughly understand that to each individual library their collection is the most important collection in the region. Committees must represent members from each type of library and each members vote or opinion should have equal weight.

People must be well informed in order to make wise decisions, so an element of the project leaders duties include attempting to put everyone at the same level of expertise and understanding.

Contact Person: Sandra Isaacson, North Country Library Cooperative, Olcott Plaza, Suite 110, 820 North 9th Street, Virginia, MN 55792, 218/741-1907, FAX 218/741-1907.

Central Minnesota Libraires Exchange (CMLE) Automation

Contact person:	Patricia Peterson
Address:	Central Minnesota Libraries Exchange
	c/o Learning Resources Center
	St. Cloud State University
	St. Cloud, MN 56301
Phone #:	612/255-2950

Project Description: CMLE makes available microfiche catalogs of three of the larger libraries — St. Cloud State University, Great River Regional Library (St. Cloud), and East Central Regional Library (Cambridge). All CMLE member libraries may make ILL requests using these catalogs. In addition, each CMLE member has been assigned a bar code and password, which enables them to access the St. Cloud State University catalog (PALS) from their own libraries. They may search the collections of all libraries in the State University System that participate in PALS. Members provide their own computers, modems, and telephone lines. If members are unable to locate citations, they can use CMLE back-up reference. There are no charges for membership, ILL or back-up reference.

Participants: Check one

___ School buildings within a district
_x_ School libraries within a library cooperative or system
___ School library (ies) with public libraries
___ School library (ies) with other types of libraries
___ State level or statewide project
___ Other (specify)

Type of Project: Check all that apply

___ Development of bibliographic database(s)
___ Shared online catalog
___ Shared circulation system
___ CD-ROM, optical disk or microform catalogs
_x_ Interlibrary loan telecommunication systems
_x_ Other automated system: dial access

Central Minnesota Libraries Exchange (CMLE)
Retrospective Conversion Project

Contact person: Patricia Peterson
Address: Central Minnesota Libraries Exchange
c/o Learning Resources Center
St. Cloud State University
St. Cloud, MN 56301
Phone #: 612/255-2950

Project Description: CMLE is assisting smaller member libraries, including approximately 30 schools, with retrospective conversion with the ultimate goal being a regional database. Libraries send their shelflist files, and the CMLE staff uses the Laser Quest system from General Research corporation to complete the conversion. The cost to the member library/ media center is $.25/title. Most larger member libraries have completed their retrospective conversion on OCLC.

Participants: Check one

___ School buildings within a district
_x_ School libraries within a library cooperative or system
___ School library (ies) with public libraries
___ School library (ies) with other types of libraries
___ State level or statewide project
___ Other (specify)

Type of Project: Check all that apply

_x_ Development of bibliographic database(s)
___ Shared online catalog
___ Shared circulation system
___ CD-ROM, optical disk or microform catalogs
___ Interlibrary loan telecommunication systems
___ Other automated system

SMILE (Southcentral Minnesota Inter-Library Exchange)/Educational Cooperative Service Unit Automation Project

Contact person: Lucy Lowry
Address: Southcentral Minnesota Inter-Library Exchange
1610 Commerce Drive
Box 3031
Mankato, MN 56001
Phone #: 507/389-5108

Project Description: SMILE, in cooperation with the Educational Cooperative Service Unit, has begun using LaserQuest to complete the conversion of catalog records of nine school districts and one special library at the library sites. The system's goal is to obtain a union catalog software program and to merge the MARC records with those of the public library system in their PALS online catalog. Schools are expected to access the catalog on a "dial-up as needed" basis until telecommunications methods change.

Participants: Check one

___ School buildings within a district
_x_ School libraries within a library cooperative or system
___ School library (ies) with public libraries
___ School library (ies) with other types of libraries
___ State level or statewide project
___ Other (specify)

Type of Project: Check all that apply

_x_ Development of bibliographic database(s)
___ Shared online catalog
___ Shared circulation system
___ CD-ROM, optical disk or microform catalogs
___ Interlibrary loan telecommunication systems
_x_ Other automated system: dial access

NEW JERSEY

Northwest Union Catalog and Interlibrary Loan System (NUCILS)

Administration: The project is administered by the Northwest Regional Library Cooperative, a multi-type library cooperative serving the five counties of Hunterdon, Morris, Somerset, Sussex, and Warren in New Jersey.

Participants: The program serves all types of libraries. In 1990, six academic, 36 public, 43 school and eight special libraries will be active, direct participants in the union catalog and interlibrary loan program. The participating schools include 29 high schools, six middle schools, seven elementary schools and one library connected with an institution serving a school age population.

Funding: The program is funded by the cooperative, with a 1990 operating cost of approximately $49,000. Participating libraries 1) provide CD-ROM hardware and their existing MARC bibliographic records; 2) agree to provide bibliographic records for new acquisitions; and 3) agree to maintain their data by providing change and delete records.

The cooperative has contracted with Auto-Graphics, Inc. for production of the union catalog on CD-ROM, for IMPACT catalog access software to access the bibliographic database, and for the IMPACT interlibrary loan module for electronic telecommunication of requests and responses. Telecommunications costs for the electronic mail vendor, Compuserve, and included in the contract with Auto-Graphics. Auto-Graphics has worked with Compuserve on the scripting and adaptation of telecommunications software.

Participants may choose to maintain their records by purchasing an Auto-Graphics Catalog Maintenance Module for use in changing classification or for deletion or addition of holdings to a record already in the database. As a result, the database provides for extremely inexpensive retrospective conversion against records in the database.

Bibliographic records from sources other than OCLC are forwarded to OCLC to be added to the New Jersey Statewide Bibliographic Database on

NEW JERSEY

OCLC. Costs for the addition of these records is shared by the cooperative and the state library.

CD-ROM and telecommunications upgrades to PC equipment, for 30 libraries to be active by October 1990, has been funded under a Targeted Grant to Test Access and Use of a Subset of the Statewide Bibliographic Database . The LSCA Title III Grant, in the amount of $60,000 includes reimbursement for each participant of $1,500 for equipment, telecommunications and supplies. Fifteen schools are participating in the grant.

Goals: The primary goals of NUCILS are to facilitate resource-sharing and to provide direct patron access to a regional database. NUCILS provides each cooperative member library with the means to access information on the holdings of other libraries within the region and to initiate interlibrary loans using a microcomputer-based electronic mailbox. In addition, NUCILS supports libraries working toward the automation of cataloging, public access catalogs and circulation control by providing a convenient mechanism for creating, storing, editing, and maintaining a MARC database. As such, the regional database helps support improved services to all residents of the region and state.

Development: From the formation of the cooperative in 1986, members libraries expressed strong interest in the use of computer technologies to support resource-sharing. This interest led to the adoption of the long-range regional plan for the creation of a computerized union catalog and interlibrary loan system.

A Regional Database Task Force, formed in April 1987, studied the requirements for creation of a regional database and functionality requirements for a regional union catalog and interlibrary loan system. The "Plan for Creation of a Northwest Union Catalog and Interlibrary Loan System," issued July 7, 1987, summarizes the Task Force's findings. On December 9, 1987, the Database Task Force Review Committee recommended Auto-Graphics as vendor for the project.

The database was first issued in December 1988. A second edition issued in May 1989, consisted of 593,675 bibliographic records with 1,081,083 holdings attached. While OCLC was the primary source for records in this initial database, other sources included MARCIVE, BroDart, and Gaylord. One large county library system provided records from their DYNIX integrated automated system. The 1990 issue consists of 844,958 bibliographic records with 1,969,351 holdings attached. Fifty-five participating libraries will have holdings on the CD-ROM. Additional sources for the database include Bibliofile, HCE, and Baker & Taylor. The Morris Automated Information Network (MAIN) provided records with holdings for public libraries in Morris County as output from a Data Research Association (DRA) integrated automated system.

The database is updated and maintained with input from the participating libraries. This input is provided as tapes from OCLC for those participants who are OCLC members, as transaction tapes from the DYNEX, DRA and Gaylord Systems, as tapes from BroDart for new acquisitions, as floppy disks from libraries purchasing from Baker & Taylor, and as floppy disks from libraries using Bibliofile, the Auto-Graphics Catalog Maintenance Module, communications format.

Functions Automated: The database was developed primarily as a tool for improved interlibrary loan access to material. It can also be used for public access to catalog records in the participating library and nearby libraries. The interlibrary loan processing function is unique to the project.

Description: To meet the need for an inexpensive, distributed system for regional resource-sharing, the Northwest Regional Library Cooperative chose in 1987 to use a microcomputer-based system and CD-ROM technology.

During 1988, bibliographic data was gathered from a variety of sources, specific decisions were made regarding record content, screen displays and indexes, and equipment was installed for implementation of the system and issuance of the first disk. During this period, arrangements were concluded to allow for inclusion of all NUCILS data in the statewide OCLC database and for the transfer of requests between NUCILS libraries and other New Jersey Library Network members.

In March 1989, a professional program coordinator was added to the cooperative staff. The day-to-day administration, training and troubleshooting are managed by the regional program coordinator. Contracts and financial administration are managed by the executive director.

Special Features: A bibliographic record is located on the CD-ROM using established IMPACT PAC software. The touch of a function key results in a CD-based ILL form. Staff may add patron information, notes, etc. The touch of another function key stores the request to be mailed at the next telecommunications session. Once a day, each participating library goes to the telecommunication portion of the software. Using a menu, they batch requests waiting to be mailed, then automatically connect to Compuserve via a scripted telecommunications interface. Messages are downloaded into Compuserve mailboxes and are uploaded from the mailbox established for the participating library. The local call to a nearby Compuserve node lasts under five minutes.

Equipment Used: The software is designed for the IBM-compatible environment. In 1990, the recommended configuration for a basic ILL/CD-ROM workstation is:
  -IBM/AT Compatible Microcomputer with Monitor and Keyboard
  -286 Chip
  -MS-DOS 3.2 or above
  -640K RAM Memory Minimum
  -One 5-1/2 or 3-1/2 Removable Disk Drive
  -Hard Drive with 10MB Minimum Storage
  -Two CD-ROM Disk Drives (Sony or Hitachi)
  -2400 Baud Modem

The hardware configuration has been upgraded to meet the requirements of database and software growth. All software is the product of Auto-Graphics, Inc. Hardware may be purchased from the participant, or the participant may upgrade equipment already in use.

Interlibrary Loan and Delivery: The program is an innovative approach to the transmission of interlibrary loan requests. Data indicates that school use of interlibrary loan prior to participation was limited to minimal borrowing and no lending, while participants with holdings in the database were active as lenders as well as borrowers. Sample school year use rates for 1989-90 of 18 loaned and 251 borrowed, 83 loaned and 133 borrowed were reported by tow high schools. One middle school reported 71 loaned and 108 borrowed. From January - May 1990, 2,523 items were lent by the 43 participating libraries.

Under this program, requests are placed electronically and answered the next day. Books are delivered via a regional courier service. Libraries with fax machines can request periodical articles via fax by using the regional print list of serial holdings or the state microfiche version of the New Jersey Union List of Serials. For this service, a blank electronic request form is used.

Successes: The cooperative staff has effectively managed rapid growth of the database and the participant group. At the same time, effective training tools and communications vehicles have been developed.

This success is reflected in the acceptance of the program by school librarians. In 1989-90, elementary and middle schools began to join high schools as participants. Acceptance by private and parochial schools has also been significant.

An unexpected impact of the project has been a tremendous increase in retrospective conversion by school libraries which formerly had no machine-readable records. It is estimated that approximately 79,000 new records were created within the first year.

The cooperative was the Beta Test Site for the Auto-Graphics IMPACT Interlibrary Loan Module. Activities connected with "debugging" telecommunications operations have been simplified by the responsive attitude of vendor and participants alike.

The project has successfully met the goal of resource-sharing on a Regional basis. In addition, participant projections have been exceeded.

Problems: The most significant problems have been with telecommunications. They have been solved and managed by establishing our credibility with the vendor's representatives and working directly with them to identify specific needed changes. For example: Due to user documentation of difficulties, the programmer was able to increase the speed of connection to telecommunications and the accuracy of file designations to avoid "invalid parameters" messages which were an initial source of frustration to users.

Advice to Others: One person should serve as the conduit for day-to-day interaction between vendor and participants. This person needs to be computer literate, to able to dispel computer fears and to be adept at encouraging people new to computer technology to ask questions and become computer comfortable. The person must be flexible in his/her approach to training and open in his/her ability to communicate enthusiasm for the program.

Regular written and verbal communications with participants should be included in any plans for project administration.

Future: Current plans call for issuance of the CD-ROM database on an annual basis. Participants have indicated an interest in semi-annual issues if funds become available.

Contact Persons: Keith Michael Fiels or Diane Macht Solomon, 908/879-2442.

Publications:
Kelsey, Ann L. and Keith Michael Fiels. "CD-ROM and ILL," Computers in Libraries '90: Proceedings of the 5th Annual Computers in Libraries Conference. Edited by Nancy Meliin Nelson. Westport, CT; London: Meckler, 1990.

Database Task Force. Northwest Regional Library Cooperative Plan for Creation of a Northwest Union Catalog and Interlibrary Loan System. Draft. Chester, NJ: Northwest Regional Library Cooperative. July 7, 1987.

Regional Database Task Force Review Committee. Report and Recommendations. Chester, NJ: Northwest Regional Library Cooperative. December, 1987.

South Jersey Union Catalog and ILL System

Contact person: Karen Hyman
Address: South Jersey Regional Library Cooperative
    Midway Professional Center, Suite 102
    8 N. White House Pike
    Hammonton, NJ 08037
Phone #:   609/561-4646

Project Description: The South Jersey Regional Library Cooperative has a CD-ROM based union catalog and electronic mail interlibrary loan system linking 35 academic, public, school, and special libraries in southern New Jersey.

Participants: Check one

___ School buildings within a district
_x_ School libraries within a library cooperative or system
___ School library (ies) with public libraries
___ School library (ies) with other types of libraries
___ State level or statewide project
___ Other (specify)

Type of Project: Check all that apply

_x_ Development of bibliographic database(s)
___ Shared online catalog
___ Shared circulation system
_x_ CD-ROM, optical disk or microform catalogs
_x_ Interlibrary loan telecommunication systems
___ Other automated system

NEW YORK

Broome-Delaware-Tioga BOCES School Library System

Administration: The School Library System (SLS) is administered through the Division of Educational Communications at the Broome-Delaware-Tioga Board of Cooperative Education Services (BOCES). It was one of the pilot networks in New York, commencing operation in 1979. By 1984 a similar network was started in each of the 41 BOCES areas and five Big City districts in the state.

Participants: The system coordinates library services, including database development, for 69 public school and four nonpublic school libraries. It services 39,000 students in grades K-12 and 3,500 teachers and administrators. Cooperative arrangements have been undertaken in conjunction with six other school library systems in the central part of the functions, part three below.

Funding: The funding for the SLS is provided by state legislation. The current annual allocation of $87,000 is determined by a formula based on enrollment, size of geographic region, number of districts, and a base grant. It must provide for a myriad of system services in addition to an automated database.

The total SLS staff consists of one professional school library media specialist with school administrative certification, one full-time, and one part-time library clerk/typist. Part-time and/or temporary input typists are hired as the work flow and budget dictate.

The automation budget has been supplemented by both Regional Automation Funding (state money which flows through regional multi-type library systems) and LSCA (federal Library Services and Construction Act Funds).

In the Broome BOCES, schools commenced contracting for complete retrospective conversion in 1989. Six building collections were completed in seven months in preparation for the selection of automated circulation/catalog systems. These schools will receive BOCES aid from the state for a percentage of the amount which each has paid. Each district's aid ratio is unique, since it is based on a number of factors, which vary from district to district.

Due to the low-budget status in 1990-91, schools will also pay to have their current acquisitions entered into the system's database in MARC format. The service to be provided for participating schools will also include a CD-ROM or COM Catalog of the whole database.

In 1989-90 the 35 schools that are equipped with CD-ROM hardware purchased an updated CD-ROM of the merged database of seven SLSs. The cost was $90 per disc.

Goals: The goals of the SLS are:

To develop a database in MARC format that can be used to produce off-line products, such as COM catalogs and CD-ROMs.

To create an awareness among participating schools of new technologies, which have potential benefits for school library media centers.

To support schools and provide coordination as school library media centers plan toward the implementation of automated circulation/catalog systems.

Other goals of this SLS will be shared upon request.

Database Development: Brodart was selected as the vendor in 1980 as a result of a bid for the production of a COM catalog. Most input has been completed at the local site, with Brodart contracted to complete input only when necessary.

The input method has changed with technological advances. For three years the now-antiquated procedure of typing with OCR (optical character recognition) elements in electric typewriters was used. Scan sheets were mailed to Brodart weekly, while Brodart responded with printouts of records entered and records that needed additional decisions. Following that process Brodart's Microcheck software was used on microcomputers. The input was easier, but dealing with the printouts Brodart returned was equally laborious.

In 1987 the SLS contracted for online services, using Brodart's Interactive Access software. With this method the input person has immediate knowledge of the contents of records in the LC MARC database, Brodart MARC and a number of online customers' databases. Printouts are not used, since decisions are made at the terminals.

When the seven SLSs merged databases in 1988 to conserve online storage costs, it was agreed that each would maintain level k MARC cataloging.

The database is currently maintained online. Schools send copies of catalog cards, with the Library of Congress number and/or ISBN printed or written on them. Likewise, as they withdraw resources from the collection they send copies of those cards also.

Functions automated: Conversion to MARC format is only one function automated. This SLS also is implementing automated means for these functions:

Union List of Periodicals within the BOCES area is maintained on a microcomputer, using PFS Professional File software.

OCLC Group Access service is used to search and to request resources needed on interlibrary loan outside of the BOCES region.

OCLC entries of periodical holdings have been completed and are maintained by the South Central Regional Research Library Council, a multi-type system in which this SLS is a member. Annually printed lists of the holdings of the seven SLS within SCRLC are ordered and distributed to schools.

An electronic bulletin board (Library Link) is hosted by BOCES Ed Comm. It is used for interlibrary loan; film, video, and microcomputer software requests; and messages to BOCES and schools. PC Board software is used.

Film, videorecording, laser-disc, and multimedia entries are entered in a separate database using Brodart Interactive Access. All MARC records were done using original cataloging to maintain our own summaries and subject headings. A CD-ROM, of this database, is produced annually.

The SLS works closely with the Film/Video service in the Division of Ed Comm, which uses the Tek Data Media Management system to book and catalog resources. These entries are not in MARC format. SLS resources, which are booked for schools in advance (puppets, literature-related stuffed animals, library and reading promotional posters, audio visual kits, and CD-ROM software) are implementing use of this system also.

Database searching is done using BRS online services and Silverplatter ERIC on CD-ROM.

Local university and public library databases are searched using Smartcom and Kermit telecommunications software.

Internal BOCES electronic mail, wordprocessing, spreadsheets, etc. are available on a Data General minicomputer system. This is tied into an IBM mainframe for access to the statewide electronic telecommunications network, Technology Network Ties (TNT).

PFS Professional File software is used to record interlibrary loan transactions and calculate statistics at the SLS office.

Description:

1980 - Input of records for resources purchased by schools from September 1978 forward was started using OCR elements and scan sheets.

1982 - The first COM Catalog (microfiche) was produced and placed in each school library.

1983 - Microcheck software used for data input.

1983 - 1989 - Complete retrospective conversion done in selected subject areas.

1985 - Periodical holdings entered in OCLC.

1986 - Started using OCLC Group Access for interlibrary loan outside of the Broome BOCES area.

1986 - First regional school library COM Catalog was produced by seven SLSs. Records from over 300 schools were included. Six of the BOCES SLS used Brodart as their utility and one used OCLC.

1987 - Interactive Access online software used for input.

1987 - Electronic bulletin board installed.

1988 - First CD-ROM produced by six SLSs.

1990 - Complete retrospective conversion done for six school libraries.

1990 - Updated CD-ROM produced by seven SLSs. It contains approximately 255,000 records with 646,000 holdings.

1990 - Periodical holdings entered in Brodart database.

Special features: New York's organization of school libraries into systems, using BOCES pre-established areas of cooperative service, facilitated networking.

As schools in this SLS work toward the installation of automated circulation/catalog systems, a three-phase plan is being followed.

Phase I - Retrospective Conversion.

Phase II - Selection and installation of automated circulation/catalog systems.

Phase III - Connection to statewide TNT telecommunication network.

Equipment used: Brodart's Interactive Access System software is used with Telex 476L terminals and a 4800 baud Racal-Milgo modem. The CD-ROMs are used in Hitachi or Amdek CD-ROM drives with IBM or compatible microcomputers. Hardware and software for other automated procedures, listed under "functions" above, will be discussed upon request.

Interlibrary Loan and Delivery: Requests mushroomed upon receipt of the first COM Catalog and again when the first CD-ROM was placed in schools. The CD-ROM features a built-in interlibrary loan form, which has saved much typing time and improved accuracy.

Schools are responsible for their own delivery to and from the BOCES Division of Ed Comm. Seventy percent of the building increased delivery from two days a week to daily during the year the CD-ROM was placed in use.

Successes: Overall, the SLS goals have been exceeded. When the database project started, CD-ROMs had not been marketed, but the use of MARC records from the onset enabled the transition to this new off-line product with no problems. The users in our schools have been very pleased with both the COM Catalog and CD-ROM. After using the search strategies available with the Brodart LePac CD-ROM, library media specialists have very sophisticated criteria for an automated catalog system.

Problems: The chief problem is funding. It has been temporarily resolved by charging schools for complete retrospective conversion, addition of current acquisitions to the database, and CD-ROMs.

The State Education Department has permitted both public and school library systems to select their own vendors, with the stipulation that MARC format be used. This provides a great deal of flexibility and freedom of choice, but leads to complications as libraries look toward linking and making connections. Much time and money have been consumed at the state level writing guidelines, but no real practical testing or assistance has been available.

The merged database of seven SLSs has no written contract. This is undoing cooperative relationships as systems discontinue service with Brodart, for financial reasons, and leave their records and holdings in the database.

When the project started in 1979, there were few school libraries which were doing anything comparable. The director of another pilot system in New York in 1979 warned us, "The pioneer is the one running with the arrow in his back." We're still running; some days the arrow feels more uncomfortable than others, but it's worth the pain.

New York

Political struggles involving compatibility of automated circulation/catalog systems with the statewide TNT system are slowing the process of selecting a vendor for this phase.

Advice to others:

Never accept a system that does not implement MARC records.

Don't rush the decision process. Spend much time in the planning and research phase.

Take advantage of other libraries' experiences.

Invest in a high quality, reliable crystal ball.

Future: The planning is in place for the selection of a common circulation/catalog system. We are waiting for the BOCES Regional Computer Center to test several software packages for compatibility with the statewide TNT system.

More training will be done with library media specialists to enable them to upload interlibrary loan requests to the system's electronic bulletin board without re keying data.

We will continually survey component school libraries' needs and search for means of meeting these needs more efficiently and cost effectively.

Contact person: Janet Bohl, Director, School Library System and Adminstrative Coordinator, Instructional Support Services, Broome-Delaware-Tioga BOCES, 421 Upper Glenwood Road, Binghamton, NY 13905-1699, 607/729-9301 X603.

Publications:
Bohl, Janet. "We Thought We Could..., a Comparison of Pilot and Permanent School Library Systems", <u>Bookmark,</u> (from the New York State Library), vol. 44, no. III, Spring 1986, pp. 152-158.

NEW YORK

Bohl, Janet and LaPier, Cynthia. "CD-ROMs Go to School," in <u>Public Access CD-ROMs in Libraries: Case Studies</u>, edited by L. Stewart, K. Chiang and B. Coons. Meckler, 1990, pp. 157-164.

NORTH CAROLINA

Neuse Regional Library/Lenoir County Schools

Contact person:	John Jones
Address:	Neuse Regional Library
	Box 510 North Queen Street
	Kinston, NC 28501
Phone #:	919/527-7066
Contact person:	Sue Rogers
Address:	Lenoir County Schools
	Route 2
	Kinston, NC 28501
Phone #:	919/523-4100

Project Description: Three high schools from two public school districts and one private school have joined forces with their regional public library to provide greater service to students. A fourth high school is due to be added in September 1990. The public library staff uses Library Corporation's Intelligent Catalog, provides centralized processing for the schools, and has placed copies of the CD-ROM Catalog in the four high schools. When students locate the material references they need, the request is forwarded to the public library.   Available articles or references are then faxed to the school library media center. LSCA monies have funded this phase.

Participants: Check one

___ School buildings within a district
___ School libraries within a library cooperative or system
_x_ School library (ies) with public libraries
___ School library (ies) with other types of libraries
___ State level or statewide project
___ Other (specify)

Type of Project: Check all that apply

___ Development of bibliographic database(s)
___ Shared online catalog
___ Shared circulation system
_x_ CD-ROM, optical disk or microform catalogs
_x_ Interlibrary loan telecommunication systems
___ Other automated system

NORTH DAKOTA

EASYLINK, ODIN, BACL

Contact person: Val Morehouse
Address: Bismarck Public School District
400 East Avenue E
Bismarck, ND 58501
Phone #: 701/221-3404

Project Description: The school district is moving into cooperative automation on several fronts. Three junior high schools and two senior high schools use EASYLINK electronic mail for statewide interlibrary loan and have dial access to Online Dakota Information Network (ODIN), an online catalog of the major resource sharing libraries. The goal is to add the elementary schools and to prepare for a shared online catalog with BACL, the Bismarck Area Cooperating Libraries.

Participants: Check one

___ School buildings within a district
___ School libraries within a library cooperative or system
___ School library (ies) with public libraries
_x_ School library (ies) with other types of libraries: academic, public
___ State level or statewide project
___ Other (specify)

Type of Project: Check all that apply

_x_ Development of bibliographic database(s)
_x_ Shared online catalog
___ Shared circulation system
___ CD-ROM, optical disk or microform catalogs
_x_ Interlibrary loan telecommunication systems
_x_ Other automated system: dial access

OREGON

Eastern Oregon School Libraries Network

Administration: This project is administered by the EOSLN Steering Committee, composed of one member from each school district involved. A project director manages the day-to-day business at the direction of the steering committee. Hermiston School District is the fiscal manager of network funds.

Participants: EOSLN has 31 individual schools, mostly junior and senior high schools, as members. These represent 29 school districts in nine counties of sparsely populated eastern Oregon. The student population served totals approximately 21,000.

Funding: Major funding for this project was provided by a private foundation grant from Fred Meyer Charitable Trust, Inc., for $121,000. There are no paid staff members. We do contract with Umatilla County Special Library District for some cataloging and computer software maintenance and licensing services. Each school site will be eventually charged for ongoing operations and annual remastering of the CD-ROM catalog at a rate of about $500 per site, depending on the size of each library collection.

Goals: Our main goal is to eventually include all school districts in eastern Oregon in the network. We are also submitting a grant request for FAX machines at each school library.

Database Development: GRC Laserquest was the primary tool used to build our database. All school library's shelflists had to be retroconverted to build the database. Records are stored on a Dynix library automation software system owned by Umatilla County Special Library District, and a Marcive CD-ROM disc will be mastered once a year for distribution to the school libraries. All records will eventually be full MARC records.

Functions Automated: Besides the electronic BBS and ILL ordering system, only the CD-ROM Public Access Catalog function is fully automated at all sites. Some schools have also automated circulation functions with their own selected software (Follett, Columbia, Molli, etc.) Some schools have dial access to the Dynix online catalog as well.

Description: Planning for the project began in the fall of 1988. Grant funds were awarded in June 1989. The hardware contract was awarded to Computerland of Pendleton in November 1989. Retroconversion of records began in 1989 and is still on-going. The first edition of the Marchive CD-ROM public access catalog will be distributed in October 1990, with 100,000 records. We hope to have a total of 250,000 records for our second edition of the catalog in October 1991. We use a PC-based BBS system developed by Eastern Oregon State College Library for electronic mail and interlibrary loan requests. The CD-ROM catalog also includes records from the Eastern Oregon Library Network, of which we are a member, adding another 14 public, three special, and one academic library's holdings.

Special Features: Unique features of our project include a joint database of the holdings of school, public, academic and special libraries of eastern Oregon. Our written agreement is unique in that it requires participating libraries to honor interlibrary requests when possible, read their mail on the BBS daily and instruct their students and teachers in the use of the system. We have interlibrary loan agreements with public as well as school libraries and local ESD courier services are used whenever possible. Many schools also have dial access to the Eastern Oregon Library Network Dynix system, as well as their own CD-ROM Marcive catalog. Short records can be loaded directly into the Dynix system from many school sites, and later overlayed with a complete MARC record.

Equipment Used: Each school library was furnished with an Epson Equity II+ microcomputer with a 40MB hard drive; a Hitachi internal CD-ROM drive, printer, modem, and color monitor; and Microsoft Works word processing, database, and telecommunications software.

Interlibrary Loan or Delivery: Interlibrary loans between school libraries and between school and public libraries increased greatly. Previously, there was very little happening here, and no formal agreements. We use a combination of delivery methods including E.S.D. courier services, state library courier, FAX and mail. No shipping fees are charged by any library for interlibrary loans.

Successes: Our greatest success was probably the hope and motivation our grant award gave to the 31 school librarians who had feared that technological progress was passing them by because of lack of funds. We received very favorable comments from the superintendents of participating schools. The Eastern Oregon School Library Network is now an organized force to further school library cooperation and networking. We believe our project met or exceeded our original goals.

Problems: Our major initial problem, funding, was solved by writing a grant proposal which was accepted by Fred Meyer Charitable Trust, a major Oregon foundation. Additional funding for other schools that wish to join the network is a continuing problem, however. Many of these schools are waiting for their own small grant requests, or will have to provide their own funding.

Another problem was providing assistance and in-service training to school librarians who had no or little previous computer experience and were very widespread over a vast geopgraphic area. Several training sessions were held, and a lot of long-distance telephone calls, neighbor-helping-neighbor, and occasional site visits by the project director or the computer vendor assisted these librarians.

Advice to others: Keep school superintendents well-informed about all stages of the project and stress the need for their cooperation and support. Allow twice as much time as you think the project will take. Consider hiring a library automation consultant, they will probably save you more money than their fee and their knowledge and experience will be invaluable to you. Develop a working written agreement for all libraries in the project specifically detailing their rights and responsibilities. Written contracts with hardware and software vendors need to be very carefully thought out and very specific—go slow and careful here, allowing plenty of time for negotiations.

OREGON

Future: We hope to eventually be able to include every school library in the region that would like to join in our network. This will depend primarily upon available funding and the desire of the local school librarian to participate.

Contact Persons: Mike Duncanson, Project Director, 503/567-9584, or Ken Reading, Umatilla County Special Library District Coordinator, 503/276-6449.

Publications:
Hunt, Sadie. "Resource Sharing in Eastern Oregon: EOSLN Builds CD-ROM Catalog." Interchange: Journal of the Oregon Educational Media Association, Winter, 1990.

PENNSYLVANIA

ACCESS PENNSYLVANIA

Administration: ACCESS PENNSYLVANIA is a compact laser disc database that contains bibliographic information of more than 11 million holdings of 566 school, public and academic libraries. The program is administered by the Pennsylvania Department of Education, State Library, School Library Media Services Division.

Participants: ACCESS PENNSYLVANIA, an agenda for knowledge and information through libraries, was established in 1984 and included a component to bring school libraries into the statewide system of resource sharing.

The 1990 database will contain information about the holdings of the following libraries: 155 public, 350 school, 21 academic, 11 university, nine community college, six special, two government, and 28 regional instructional materials centers. Libraries are required to join the project by responding to Requests for Applications, a competitive grant process, only multi-library type proposals are accepted.

Funding: The project, which started in 1984, was funded in its first year with Library Services and Construction Act monies. Starting in 1985, a separate line item in the governor's budget was established and provided $200,000 to be used specifically for the costs involved in converting the information about the holdings of school libraries into machine readable form. This line item has gradually been increased to the current level of $500,000. Approximately $250,000 of LSCA funds is used each year to cover expenses involved in adding the records of public and academic libraries to the database as well as for database creation and processing cost. LSCA funds are also used to offset some of the interlibrary loan expenses. Local libraries use local monies to purchase equipment and to keep their holdings updated.

Goals: The goals of the project are:

To establish a network to share resources.

To improve each student's information-management skills.

Pennsylvania

To increase access to information by students and teachers.

To improve the management of the school library.

To provide access to a union catalog of school, public, academic, and special libraries.

Database Development: It was determined that Pennsylvania needed a vendor who could (1) convert the holdings of school libraries into machine readable form, (2) strip information about the holdings of public and academic libraries from MARC tapes, (3) combine all of this data into one database, and (4) create a union catalog on compact laser disc that would permit access by title, author, subject, location, format, or any word. Brodart Inc. was chosen as the vendor.

Brodart sends a van to each school and helps the school librarian pack the shelf cards into boxes. These are then taken to Brodart in Williamsport, PA where they are converted into MARC format. Two copies of each school's holdings are produced on MARC tape; one is sent to the school to be used as input for automating library management functions, while the other is sent to the project's consultant, Dr. James Fogarty, of Intermediate Unit 29, where the tapes are checked for accuracy. Any tapes found which do not meet the project's criteria are returned to Brodart for reprocessing.

All libraries are required to update their records once a year. Schools send copies of their adds, changes, and deletes to the project consultant who checks for accuracy and then forwards them to Brodart. Academic and public libraries are required to send their updates on MARC tape directly to Brodart.

Functions to be Automated: While the primary intent of the project was to create a union catalog of multi-library types, a secondary benefit was realized. The same MARC tape that was created for each school is used to automate school library management functions. Schools determine which of the approved library management software vendors they want to work with to automate their library. The vendor then uses the MARC tape to provide the records needed and embeds the bar code numbers directly into the records. They then can print out the bar codes in shelf order which helps to speed up the time consuming task of automating a library.

Pennsylvania

After the user searches the database and finds an item he or she wants to borrow, and interlibrary loan form can be automatically called up with the touch of one key. The form is completely filled in with the exception of two fields: the date the item is needed and whether or not they are willing to pay any additional costs which may be involved. The form provides the complete address of both the lending and the borrowing library, which can then be used as labels for the packages of materials. The ILL form can also be downloaded in an ASCII format for transmission on an electronic mail system. Many ACCESS PENNSYLVANIA cosortiums have installed E mail systems to facilitate interlibrary loan. In addition, records may also be downloaded into MicroLIF format and added to the school's automated circulation system.

Description: Planning for the project began in 1984 and the first compact laser disc was up and running by September 1986. The automated interlibrary loan component was added in 1988. The database is currently housed on four compact laser discs subdivided by date. The first set of two contains the holdings from 1972 to the current date, all serials, and all information about the audio visual holdings of the regional instructional media centers. The second set holds materials which are pre-1972.

Special Features: One of the most appreciated special features of the project is that school librarians are not required to do their own conversion. It is projected that this feature has saved hundreds of hours of work and has allowed school librarians more time to work with students and teachers.

Other libraries in the state that wish to pay for their own retrospective conversion may benefit from the same negotiated state price and enter the project without having to go through the competitive bid process.

The project has created a network of multi-library types which has encouraged participants to get involved with one another in other projects such as cooperative collection development and telefax networks.

Equipment Used: Only project approved systems may be used. Currently, participants may choose from either the IBM PS/2 Model 30-286 with 1024K, 1.44MB disk and 30MB fixed disk, or the Tandy 1000 TL/2 with memory expansion 128K to 768K, and a 20 meg hard card. Libraries in consortiums that will use electronic mail for interlibrary loan are also required to purchase a modem as well. Both systems are required to have MS-DOS extensions and two compact laser disc readers. Participants may take advantage of a statewide microcomputer bid list if they desire.

Interlibrary Loan and Delivery: Interlibrary loan delivery can be accomplished in various ways. First, the state library provides LSCA monies to support a major portion of an Interlibrary Delivery System within the state. Secondly, each consortium was required to establish its own local delivery system among its libraries. In addition, many informal arrangements for the delivery of materials have been made.

Successes: The database has opened up a world of resources to students and teachers and has impacted the teaching/learning process. Students are now using sources of information which they did not have access to before the creation of the database. Teachers are reporting that the quality of research papers is improving and that many students are demonstrating a broader knowledge base of their research and are using new sources of information in obtaining divergent opinions about the topic they are investigating.

The creation of the database has demonstrated the importance of state leadership. This is a project which would have been extremely difficult for schools to do on their own. The manner in which the database was created did not impinge upon the precious time that school librarians have to spend with students. For this, the school librarians are extremely grateful.

The project has helped to break down the barriers that had previously existed among libraries of different types. In addition to the benefits provided by resource sharing, a network of friends has been established which has enriched all who have been involved.

The state legislators have been involved in the project from its inception. As schools were accepted into the project, many librarians wrote letters to their legislators, thanking them for their support and inviting them to visit the school for a demonstration of the benefits of the database and a picture taking session. Public and academic librarians also kept their legislators informed about their involvement in the project and also provided press coverage when legislators visited the library. These types of activities have helped to maintain the line item in the annual state budget which provides the major portion of the funding needed for the project.

All schools in the project now have their library management functions automated. Schools who have not been accepted into the project to date are now having full MARC records created when they automate library management functions. This enables them to join the project without having to wait for additional state funding.

Academic libraries are enjoying the additional public relations as a result of participating in the project. As students open materials they borrow from academic libraries, they often find book markers or brochures about the institution which provided the resources. As a result, students and parents are becoming more aware of the programs and services which are available at their local universities.

Problems: In the beginning, some non-MARC records were accepted which caused technical problems. We no longer accept any non-MARC records.

The size of the database has grown from one compact laser disc to four. It is currently subdivided by date. After the end of the 1989-90 year, an analysis will be made to determine whether this is the best subdivision of the database or whether some other division would be more useful.

Many more schools want to join the database than we can accommodate each year. This can be discouraging to schools. However, if the school purchases the equipment, and commits to joining the project as soon as monies become available, it is given a copy of the database and is permitted to join the interlibrary loan network.

The quality of the database is improving each year. However, there are still some areas of the database which need attention. Name and subject authority control have been partially applied to the database, but because of the large number of types of libraries and forms of authority used, it is not possible to implement a thorough authority process.

Schools would like to update their holdings via floppy disk rather than using shelflist cards. Work is still being done in this area to determine whether such a request can be accommodated.

PENNSYLVANIA

Linking Information Needs - Technology, Education, Libraries (LIN-TEL)

Administration: LIN-TEL is a statewide online searching network designed to provide students and school librarians with access to commercial online databases. The program is administered by the Pennsylvania Department of Education, State Library, School Library Media Services Division.

Participants: LIN-TEL was created in February 1983 in order to assist school librarians integrate online searching skills into the information-management curriculum of the schools. Pennsylvania was the first state in the nation to institute a statewide online searching network that included public schools.

Funding: Funding was originally provided by a combination of National Institute of Education (NIE) and state funds. During the second year, Library Service and Construction Act (LSCA) funds supported the network. In 1986, the Pennsylvania Department of Education assumed the major responsibility of funding the network.

A master account was established with the online vendor, BRS Information Technologies. Each site is assigned an amount of money for online searching cost based on the number of years they have participated in the network. The master account concept permits each site to have their costs for online searching deducted directly at BRS and avoids the problem of negotiating separate contracts with all the schools involved in the project.

The Pennsylvania Department of Education assumes a predetermined amount of the online searching costs for a period of three years. Each site is then encouraged to acquire its own password with BRS and assume its own online searching costs. These sites are then known as "Lin-Dependent" network members.

Goals: LIN-TEL has four main goals:

To make online database searching available to students as another method of information retrieval.

To make research/resource gathering integral to the school library media curriculum.

To provide local education agencies with direct access to online databases of professional literature which they can draw upon to make informed decisions about administrative and curricular matters.

To stimulate the exchange of information among school districts, intermediate units, the Pennsylvania Department of Education, public, academic and special libraries, and other educational institutions.

Database Development: BRS Information Technologies is the vendor LIN-TEL provides to its members. All the databases which are made available by the vendor can be accessed by LIN-TEL members.

Functions Automated: The physical activities involved in searching for materials manually can now be performed electronically. In addition, LIN-TEL members can use the electronic mail system to send interlibrary loan requests or messages to other members.

Description: The original schools who were invited to join LIN-Tel in its first year of operation were of operation were identified by a review of the old ESEA Title IVB files to locate schools that purchased microcomputer equipment which could be used for online searching. In addition, the rosters of 12 microcomputer workshops were cross-referenced in an attempt to identify school librarians who would be willing to get involved in the project. Contacts were then made with these two groups so that the LIN-TEL network could be initiated as quickly as possible. When schools decide they would like to join the network, they are placed on a waiting list and are added to the project as funding permits.

Librarians receive three days training in online searching and the utilization of the BRS Search System. They are then expected to integrate online searching into the school curriculum. To support this activity, PENNSYL-VANIA ONLINE: A Curriculum Guide for School Library Media Centers was published in 1985. It is anticipated that the revised version of this document will be ready for dissemination by September 1990.

PENNSYLVANIA

Special Features: In order to recognize the students who are becoming competent online searchers, the "Outstanding Student Searcher Contest" was created. After each LIN-TEL site holds a local contest, the best online search is forwarded to the Pennsylvania Department of Education. Online searching specialists from the Department then choose the best three searches. These students, and their school librarians, are then the department's guests at the Pennsylvania School Librarians Conference where a run-off contest is held. The students each receive small cash awards and certificates. The first place student receives a trophy while the first place school receives a plaque for its trophy case.

A LIN-TEL newsletter, which includes helpful searching hints, training announcements, success stories, and lots of how-to information, is published every two months. Two user meetings are conducted annually where participants receive advanced training, preview various related products, and develop online searching curriculum.

Equipment Used: Members must commit to providing a microcomputer or terminal, modem, and a printer, as well as an outside direct telephone line. In addition, a communications package, such as Hayes Smartcom, Crosstalk, or Procomm must be purchased.

Interlibrary Loan and Delivery: Interlibrary loan is an important part of LIN-TEL. After students execute an online search and identify the articles needed, they then send an electronic message to their document retrieval site. Three universities, Mansfield, Clarion, and Millersville, are under contract by the Pennsylvania Department of Education to provide LIN-TEL members with copies of the ERIC microfiche or copies of the journal articles. When the journal is not available at the document retrieval site, the message can be forwarded to the Pennsylvania Department of Education's Resource Center.

Successes: LIN-TEL has expanded access to resources beyond the walls of the school library. Students are not only learning the physical and mental skills necessary to conduct an online search, they are becoming more cognizant of the range of resources and materials which are available for their research needs.

PENNSYLVANIA

The online searching contest has brought recognition to the school librarians and they are now being viewed as the information broker of their schools. Many LIN-TEL members report that since they got involved in using technology in their libraries, their budgets have actually increased.

LIN-TEL provided four of the 34 Philadelphia high schools with access to online database searching. After reviewing the impact that this activity had on student achievement, Dr. Constance Clayton, superintendent of the school district of the City of Philadelphia, provided the necessary funding to include all 34 schools in the project. This included purchasing all necessary hardware and software and providing funds for online search time.

Problems: One of the major problems has been the lack of sufficient time for the school librarians to develop online searching skills in order to become proficient enough to feel comfortable with integrating the concept into the curriculum.

However, Pennsylvania Department of Education staff is available for technical assistance and can be reached by electronic mail, telephone, or surface mail.

When LIN-TEL staff recognizes that there is a problem in a particular region, arrangements are made to provide supplemental training.

Advice to Others:

Use only MARC records. Do not accept any non-MARC records in the database.

As participants become more technology oriented, they will expect more and more in less and less time.

Select your vendors carefully and maintain constant communications. Pennsylvania feels that one of the reasons the project has been so successful is that the vendor has been kept well-informed about all components of the project.

Cultivate the support of legislators. Without their support, funding will be extremely difficult to obtain.

PENNSYLVANIA

Assist participants in developing their local political environments. They need to understand why such support is needed and how to develop strategies to obtain it.

Provide procedure manuals for all project participants. This will reduce the number of phone calls received and will cut down on the time spent providing advisory services.

Future: Future plans include getting all libraries that have indicated a desire to join the project on the database. This will require increased funding both at the state and local level.

Incorporating more features in the software is always under consideration. The current system, however, is responding very well to the needs of the participants, so that software changes may prove to be only minor improvements transparent to the user.

Contact Person: Doris Epler, Division Director of School Library Media Services, Pennsylvania Department of Education, 333 Market Street, Harrisburg, PA 17126-0333, 717/787-6704.

Publications:
Epler, Doris M. "Networking in Pennsylvania: Technology and the School Library Media Center" Library Trends. Vol 37, n 1, Summer 1988, pp. 43-55.

Fogarty, James. "A Success Story: Library Resource Sharing", Media & Methods. Vol. 23, No. 2, November/December 1986, pp. 10-11.

Goodlin, Margaret. "Networking in Pennsylvania: An ACCESS PENN-SYLVANIA Update", PALINET News. Number 56, December, 1989, pp. 1,2 & 7.

Nesbit, Larry, Doris Epler and James Fogarty. "Building Optical Disc Collections for Schools" Media & Methods. Vol. 24, No. 2, November/December 1988, pp. 21-25.

SOUTH CAROLINA

South Carolina Public School Library Media Center Demonstration Project

Contact person:	Julie Boulware
Address:	Lexington School Districts
	6051 Wescott Road
	Columbia, SC 29212
Phone #:	803/732-8200
Contact person:	Coordinator of Media Services
	Lexington School District 2
	715 9th Street
	West Columbia, SC 29169
Phone #:	803/796-4708

Project Description: A Public School Library Media Center Demonstration Project is being carried out to determine the feasibility of school library media center participation the the South Carolina Library Network. The South Carolina Library Database is being built upon the SOLINET/OCLC database and uses hardware that is also used to manage internal functions of the state library. Three school libraries in Lexington District V have become full network participants and are placing online requests for students and faculty. The three school libraries from the School District of Oconee County have successfully automated their local libraries but have experienced difficulty in gaining access to the network due to local telecommunications problems. A third grant was made to the Lexington School District II for the automation of two school libraries. As these libraries increase their use of the network, it should provide sufficient information to determine the impact of participation by school libraries.

Participants: Check one

___ School buildings within a district
___ School libraries within a library cooperative or system
___ School library (ies) with public libraries
___ School library (ies) with other types of libraries
_x_ State level or statewide project
___ Other (specify)

SOUTH CAROLINA

Type of Project: Check all that apply

_x_ Development of bibliographic database(s)
___ Shared online catalog
___ Shared circulation system
___ CD-ROM, optical disk or microform catalogs
_x_ Interlibrary loan telecommunication systems
___ Other automated system

SOUTH DAKOTA

South Dakota Library Network

Contact person: Becky Bell
Address: South Dakota State Library
                      800 Governors Drive
                      Pierre, SD 57501
Phone #:   605/773-3131

Project Description: SDLN is a statewide automation project in South Dakota utilizing the PALS software from UNISYS. Currently the database holds over 1,000,000 records for 10 state-owned institutions, and five private academic or public libraries. Small school and public libraries have dial access to the union catalog. Planning is still underway for the process of retroconversion of the holdings of the small school and public libraries. There will probably be three levels of participation by the small school and public libraries: 1) dial access only; 2) dial access with local automation for circulation, etc. and retroconversion of holdings for the network; and 3) full network membership.

Participants: Check one

___ School buildings within a district
___ School libraries within a library cooperative or system
___ School library (ies) with public libraries
___ School library (ies) with other types of libraries
_x_ State level or statewide project
___ Other (specify)

Type of Project: Check all that apply

_x_ Development of bibliographic database(s)
_x_ Shared online catalog
_x_ Shared circulation system
___ CD-ROM, optical disk or microform catalogs
_x_ Interlibrary loan telecommunication systems
_x_ Other automated system: dial access

VERMONT

Vermont Automated Library System

Contact person: Sybil McShane
Address: Vermont Department of Libraries
109 State Street
Montpelier, VT 05602
Phone #: 802/828-3261

Project Description: VALS is an integrated online, distributed library system transparently linking the databases of the Vermont Department of Libraries, Middlebury College, University of Vermont, the Vermont State Colleges (4), and Norwich University. The holdings of 100 public libraries are scheduled to be added in spring of 1990. All of the linked databases can be searched with a single local telephone call and a single search inquiry strategy. Transactions are done online. Schools have access to the databases, but their holdings are not included. Schools must pay any necessary telecommunications.

Participants: Check one

___ School buildings within a district
___ School libraries within a library cooperative or system
___ School library (ies) with public libraries
___ School library (ies) with other types of libraries
_x_ State level or statewide project
___ Other (specify)

Type of Project: Check all that apply

___ Development of bibliographic database(s)
___ Shared online catalog
___ Shared circulation system
___ CD-ROM, optical disk or microform catalogs
_x_ Interlibrary loan telecommunication systems
_x_ Other automated system. (Access to statewide system only. Holdings not included.)

VIRGINIA

Henrico County Public Schools/Public Library Network

Administration: The program is administered by Henrico County Public Schools, Department of Instruction, Library Services, in cooperation with the Henrico County Public Library. The Data Processing Department for Henrico County government is responsible for software implementation and the initial instruction of librarians on various applications. It serves as liaison between schools and public libraries regarding program changes and modifications to reports.

Participants: The program was designed to form a network of resources among the Henrico County Public Schools and between the schools and public library. Of the 51 public schools in Henrico County, seven senior high schools, two middle schools, seven elementary schools are currently part of the network, as well as the Humanities Center, Mathematics and Science Center, and the Division Media Center. The remainder of the schools will be phased in over the next few years.

Funding: The project was begun with federal grants through the Virginia State Department of Education in the amounts of $5,000 and $15,000. The school division budget contains funding for terminals which are added each year as additional schools go online. The database is updated and maintained by one data entry clerk.

Goals:

To establish a database of the holdings of school libraries in Henrico County for the purpose of sharing resources among the schools and between the schools and the public library.

To give students access to and experience with obtaining information electronically.

To manage resources more efficiently through the utilization of automated cataloging, overdues, and bibliographic control.

To maximize use of resources and prevent unnecessary duplication by specializing collections at the seven senior high school libraries.

Virginia

Database Development: The Computer Company was selected for retrospective conversion because it was local and assistance could be obtained more conveniently. Access to and inclusion in The State of Virginia library database (CAVALIR) was also a contributing factor to our selection.

Each high school was responsible for claiming its own records online. Each library's staff searched The Computer Company's database by entering any or all of the following keys: Author, Title, ISBN, LCCN.

Following the conversion, the first three senior high schools' records were loaded from MARC tapes into the database. For monetary reasons, data from the next schools were keyed directly online. After a two-year period, we began using Bibliofile and again maintain records in MARC format.

Functions Automated: Circulation - This is an integrated system, allowing for automated circulation and an online public access catalog.

Inventory - Requires separate programming but has been implemented using a MSI PD terminal and software developed by the county data processing personnel.

Cataloging - Cataloging is accomplished through use of Bibliofile. MARC records are stored and can be downloaded to the mainframe.

Description: The senior high schools' libraries have been fully automated since 1987. A new elementary school opened in fall1988, with an automated circulation system and online catalog. Additional elementary and middle schools become part of the network yearly. We anticipate that it will be at least five years before all school libraries are part of the network.

Special Features:

Access to the public library's holdings requires only the depression of one key. It is simple to toggle back and forth to access either database.

One library card can be used at the school or at the public library.

Overdue notices are printed weekly and delivered to the schools for distribution.

A countywide electronic mail system facilitates interlibrary loan.

Special collections such as the Mathematics-Science library and the Humanities Center library are part of the database.

The holdings of the Division Media Center are part of this database and accessible to teachers either online or through printouts of special subject bibliographies.

Equipment Used: The software was purchased from the Pueblo Library System and has been modified to meet the needs of the schools and public library.

The mainframe is a UNISYS System 80, Model 20. The terminals are UNISYS SVT1120. The bar code scanner used is Compsee # GR2100 26578-580. An MSI PDT handheld terminal is used for inventory.

Interlibrary Loan or Delivery: At the present time, interlibrary loan procedures are handled via a printed form delivered by "pony" to the schools. Requested materials are delivered the same way. In the future, interlibrary loan requests will be handled by electronic mail.

Successes: Each high school has specialized collection development so that expensive reference materials need not be duplicated but are available to each student or teacher through the online capabilities of the computer terminals. Data for materials such as videotapes, sound filmstrips, etc., available from the Division Media Center has been entered into the database. An interlibrary loan system facilitates sharing these resources. In addition to this expanded collection of materials, each senior high school library has automated circulation capabilities as well as the ability to inventory and maintain management of resources. Another bonus of this system is that the public library card will give the student borrowing privileges at either the school or the Henrico County Public Library. School library cards are issued to students who do not have public library cards.

Instruction in the use of this database is integral to the comprehensive library skills program and serves as the basis for teaching search strategies, indexing skills, and for instruction in using commercial databases. The system makes possible the teaching of high-level thinking skills for accessing and evaluating information through the online public access catalog. Students are intrigued by the system and put to use indexing skills previously learned in a different context.

Automation has made establishing a catalog for new schools a simpler process. The necessity for typing and filing cards is eliminated and therefore personnel need not be employed as far in advance of opening as usual.

The preparation of bibliographies is a batch process, requires only a simple service request, and can be done overnight.

Problems: Cataloging differences were resolved as a result of librarians involved meeting together and deciding on cataloging standardization. Any major decisions regarding cataloging are a result of polling the participants. All original cataloging and data entry is handled centrally for all schools in the database.

We would prefer that local holdings come up on the screen first followed by school division holdings and then access to the public library. This search hierarchy would be less time consuming. At present, the student must locate a title, then continue the search through another screen until the holdings appear. We have not resolved this problem. The users group needs to agree to this change.

As the holdings of the elementary school libraries were added, we realized that students would have many screens to read before locating their school in the holdings record. To facilitate this search we added a "+" sign to juvenile subjects eliminating the necessity to search any secondary school (senior high and middle) records. The same is true of Division Media Center holdings which have a "#" sign appended to the subject heading.

There is no capability for keyword searching. The public library has solved this by using a CD-ROM catalog. We may be able to add our records to this. It is under consideration at this time.

VIRGINIA

Advice to Others: Always put your records in MARC format. Perhaps the particular software program may not need this information or you may feel that the detail in MARC unnecessary for your purposes. There is no "status quo" in automation. Change comes continually and a MARC record will give you the accuracy and consistency for any new program.

Future: We will continue to add the holdings of our remaining schools to our database as funds and time permit. We may find it feasible to append our holdings to the CD-ROM database now used by the public library.

Contact Person: Elizabeth K. Browning, Henrico County Public Schools, P.O. Box 23120, Richmond, VA 23223

Southside Virginia Library Network I

Contact person: Martha LeStourgeon
Address: Longwood Library
                  Longwood College
                  Farmville, VA 23901
Phone #:   804/395-2633

Project Description: The Southside Virginia Library Network, established in the fall of 1984 to improve access to all educational materials and information through the provision of resources and instruction for the residents of Southside Virginia, is expanding to enable Longwood's VTLS database resources to reach 18 additional sites. Through LSCA, funds were obtained to purchase microcomputers, modems and software to allow libraries to dial into the Longwood College library. The network consists of Longwood College, Southside Virginia Community College; Amelia, Appomattox, Buckingham, Campbell, Charlotte, Cumberland, Halifax/South Boston, Lunenburg, Mecklenburg, Nottoway, Powhatan, and Prince Edward school systems and the public libraries of Appomattox, Buckingham, Cumberland, Farmville-Prince Edward, Halifax/South Boston, Nottoway Counties and the Southside Regional Library.

Participants: Check one.

___ School buildings within a district
___ School libraries within a library cooperative or system
___ School library(ies) with public libraries
_x_ School library (ies) with other types of libraries: academic, public
___ State level or statewide project
___ Other (specify)

Type of Project: Check all that apply

___ Development of bibliographic database(s)
___ Shared online catalog.
___ Shared circulation system.
___ CD-ROM, optical disk or microform catalogs
___ Interlibrary loan telecommunication systems
_x_ Other automated system: dial access

VIRGINIA

Southside Virginia Library Network II

Contact person: Martha LeStourgeon
Address: Longwood Library
                 Longwood College
                 Farmville, VA 23901
Phone #:   804/395-2633

Project Description: Approximately eight high schools subscribe to ERIC on CD-ROM. Libraries can request the full text of documents by sending ILL requests via FAX.

Participants: Check one

___ School buildings within a district
___ School libraries within a library cooperative or system
___ School library (ies) with public libraries
_x_ School library (ies) with other types of libraries
___ State level or statewide project
___ Other (specify)

Type of Project: Check all that apply

___ Development of bibliographic database(s)
___ Shared online catalog
___ Shared circulation system
___ CD-ROM, optical disk or microform catalogs
_x_ Interlibrary loan telecommunication systems
___ Other automated system

WASHINGTON

Seven Oaks Elementary School Building Network

Contact person: Terry Wright
Address: Division of Instructional Services
North Thurston School District
305 College Street, N.E.
Lacey, WA 98506
Phone #:   206/493-9053

Project Description: Seven Oaks Elementary School, was to open September 1990, with a building-wide network, which interconnects teaching stations, the principal, the intervention specialist, the office secretaries, and the library. The network provides four major services: online catalog, word processing, electronic mail, and grade book. This allows each student to search for materials without leaving the classroom. Circulation status can be determined, and a list of materials from the card catalog could be copied into a "note home" or "sent to the librarian" request via electronic mail.

Participants: Check one

___ School buildings within a district
___ School libraries within a library cooperative or system
___ School library (ies) with public libraries
___ School library (ies) with other types of libraries
___ State level or statewide project
_x_ Other (specify) School building network

Type of Project: Check all that apply

___ Development of bibliographic database(s)
___ Shared online catalog
___ Shared circulation system
___ CD-ROM, optical disk or microform catalogs
___ Interlibrary loan telecommunication systems
_x_ Other automated system: School building network

WISCONSIN

Wisconsin Statewide Database Program (WISCAT)

Administration: The program was administered by the Department of Public Instruction, Division for Library Services, Bureau for Interlibrary Loan and Resource Sharing.

Participants: The program was intended to reach libraries of all types and sizes which were interested in sharing resources or in undertaking local automation projects requiring use of machine-readable bibliographic records.

The program currently includes approximately 700 academic, public, school, and special libraries. All major public and private 2-4 year colleges are included and most of the public universities have completed retrospective conversion. All public library system resource libraries are included and have converted most of their collections. Many smaller public, school, and special libraries are also included. Schools have either joined as districts or by individual school buildings at all levels. Branch libraries are also included.

A major effort has been made to include school libraries in this project. In 1989, over 300 school libraries were included making schools the largest group of participating libraries.

Funding: The program has been funded with Library Services and Construction Act funds since 1982. LSCA funds pay for the cost of staff and for maintaining, updating, and making the masters of the microfiche and CD-ROM version of the database. For 1989, libraries will pay about half of the cost of a microfiche copy ($300) and the full cost of a CD-ROM copy ($80). LSCA funds have also been available for retrospective conversion and libraries receiving grants receive two free copies during the grant year. LSCA funds have also been allocated to purchase CD-ROM drives for public libraries. Libraries have used local funds for equipment and staff to carry out retrospective conversion and to update the database. The program staff includes two full-time and two part-time staff members. The division is seeking state funds for the program.

WISCONSIN

Goals: The goals of the program at the onset were and continue to be:

Development of a statewide resource sharing tool.

Development of a source of machine-readable bibliographic records for libraries implementing local automation projects.

Database Development: The division contracted with Brodart to build and maintain the database. The original database was developed using OCLC archival tapes and tapes from local library automation programs, some of which were not in the MARC format. Two software packages were developed which allow libraries not using OCLC to add their holdings to records already in the database. MITINET/marc allows library staff to create original MARC records without having to learn the MARC tagging structure.

An interface which allows libraries using Bibliofile to contribute Library of Congress records has also been developed. Each library is responsible for updating records in the database using OCLC or MITINET/retro.

Functions Automated: The primary intent was to create a machine-readable database of bibliographic records and holdings to assist library staff and patrons in identifying the location of materials. The first six editions were produced on computer output microfiche (COM). The last two editions were also produced on CD-ROM. The CD-ROM edition greatly facilitates interlibrary loan and reference functions.

This program also concentrated on the development of an interlibrary loan telecommunications network. Microcomputer equipment was purchased for all public library systems and state level resource libraries. A bulletin board system was developed which allowed public library system offices and academic libraries to send requests to state level resource libraries. Seven public library systems also operate bulletin boards.

Local libraries have used records extracted from the database in local automated programs including online catalogs, circulation systems, local COM and CD-ROM catalogs, and other local systems.

WISCONSIN

Description: Planning for the project began in 1978 and the first micro-fiche catalog was produced in 1982. MITINET/retro software was developed in 1983 and MITINET/marc was first released in 1985 with a revised release available in 1989. The bulletin board system was implemented at the state level in 1985 and at the system level in 1986-87. The CD-ROM version of the catalog was produced and interfaced with the bulletin board system in 1989.

Special Features: Unique features of the program include the development of the MITINET/retro and MITINET/marc software which allows small libraries to convert their collections to MARC format. These two programs greatly facilitated the process of including holdings from small libraries in the database on an equal level as larger libraries.

Libraries can extract their records from the database at a low cost of $.005 per record and load the records into local automated systems. Division staff have worked with many vendors, including microcomputer vendors, to facilitate the process of downloading records to local systems.

The interface between the CD-ROM system and the bulletin board system allows libraries to search the CD-ROM and load data into interlibrary loan forms for transmission to other libraries via the BBS. The BBS software is supported by the division and can be installed at the system or school district level.

Equipment Used: Libraries using OCLC used standard OCLC terminals or the M300 series microcomputers. MITINET/retro and MITINET/marc were developed for the Apple II and IBM-PC microcomputers or compatibles. The Bulletin Board system operates on an IBM-PC, but libraries can send interlibrary loan files using either Apple II or IBM-PC equipment.

Interlibrary Loan or Delivery: The use of the COM and CD-ROM versions of the database provided information on the holdings of a wide variety of libraries of all sizes for the first time. This primarily affected interlibrary loan and walk-in access at the local and system level and allowed libraries to refer patrons or send more requests directly to each other. The bulletin board system made the transmission of requests possible and the process more efficient. Materials are delivered by mail, delivery van, or telefacsimile depending on the resources of the library or system.

Successes: The database created is one of the largest in both bibliographic records and holdings currently produced by a state agency. It now contains over 3.5 million bibliographic records and over 17 million library holdings. There are currently 130 CD-ROM installations with 13 installed in school libraries. The number of CD-ROM installations is expected to grow each year and the microfiche version will gradually be phased out.

School libraries have been especially enthusiastic about the ability to convert holdings to machine-readable form in order to load the records into local systems. Numerous school libraries are taking part in system level bulletin board systems with the most active installation in the Arrowhead, Nicolet, and Wisconsin Valley Library Systems.

Schools have been more effectively included in statewide planning and consulting efforts and have become more active participants in interlibrary loan an other resource sharing efforts.

The division's coordination of all processes involved in submitting records and making extractions makes it possible to include libraries with varying levels of expertise and experience. It also allows the division to develop and implement standards for input and use of hardware and software. The division converts all data created on floppy disks to tape before it is sent to the vendor greatly facilitating the update of the database.

Problems: The size of the database and the many forms of input and output caused many technical and quality control problems. Working through these with the vendor required precise documentation, communication, and testing. A quality control committee with representation from all types of libraries was appointed. Some quality control problems can only be handled through manual changes, requiring staff time.

The addition of non-MARC records to the database caused many quality control problems even though an attempt to convert them to MARC format was made.

Standards were also set for cataloging quality for records submitted using MITINET/marc and records were reviewed prior to entering them into the database. Because of the varying levels of cataloging expertise and knowledge of AACR2, this review has taken more staff time than anticipated.

Name and subject authority control have been partially applied to the database, but because of the large number of types of libraries and forms of authority used, it is not possible to implement a thorough authority control process.

The difficulty of loading MARC records into non-MARC local systems, both mini-computer and microcomputer, was underestimated. Each system has had to be treated separately and staff had to work with each vendor to work through the conversion process.

Library staff would like to be able to update the database using transactions generated by their local systems rather than using OCLC or MITINET. No solution has been found for this yet, and dual input is still necessary.

Release of software to libraries requires careful planning and documentation. A large amount of staff time has been spent in communication with libraries, development of manuals and training materials, and in development of training workshops. Software was released only for the IBM PC and Apple II computers and compatibles.

The more an automated system can do, the more people want it to do. Change has been made carefully, mostly after much testing.

Advice to Others: Include only records originally created as MARC records in the database. Machine conversion from non-MARC records regardless of the source are not satisfactory. It is important for libraries to update the database once they have added their holdings to it.

Hire staff to manage the program who are thoroughly familiar with the MARC format and AACR2 cataloging rules and who have some experience in using automated systems.

Don't underestimate the importance of developing user manuals and training materials which provide precise and accurate instructions on using all components of the system. This is especially important if a large number of libraries are to be included.

Give vendors detailed and precise instructions on the products to be produced, especially if any non-standard or custom processing is to be done. Be prepared to document problems carefully and share information with the vendor. Without this type of information, vendors are unlikely to meet your expectations.

If the program is a statewide or regional project, assign one person to coordinate communication with the vendor. This greatly facilitates problem solving and communication. Having each library communicate with a vendor will lead to a great deal of confusion.

The political environment is important for a program which involves so many different types and sizes of libraries. The need, purpose, and advantages of a program need to be continually stressed and many groups need to be informed. School librarians often need to overcome local district policies which do not always encourage sharing of materials and release time for training and participation.

Future: Future plans will involve incorporating more features into the CD-ROM product and improving the interlibrary loan interface so that library staff can access active requests, maintain statistics on interlibrary loan transactions, and refer requests (without retyping) to other libraries when the first source cannot provide the materials.

Contact Person: Sally Drew, 608/221-6161 or Mary Clark, 608/221-6179.

Publications:
Epstein, Hank. The effective use of automation in Wisconsin libraries, 1981-1985, Costa Mesa, CA, 1980. (Copies available through interlibrary loan only.)

Aveney, Brian and Sally Drew. Automated Resource Sharing: Wisconsin Spreads Its Nets, Wilson Library Bulletin, May 1983.

WISCONSIN

Bocher, Robert. MITINET: Catalog Conversion to a MARC Database, School Library Journal, March 1985.

Council on Library and Network Development, Report of the Council on Library and Network Development to the State Superintendent of Public Instruction on Automating Wisconsin Libraries, Bulletin no. 8100, Madison, WI, 1987.

IOLS '89: Proceedings of the Fourth Integrated Online Library Systems Meeting, May 10-11, 1989, New York, Learned Information, Inc.

Channel DLS, Wisconsin Division for Library Services. (Articles in many issues from 1983 to present.)

INDEX TO PROJECT TYPES

STATE LEVEL OR STATEWIDE PROJECTS
Alabama Union List of Serials
ACCESS PENNSYLVANIA
Capital City Libraries
Georgia Online Database (GOLD)
Iowa Locator
LIN-TEL
reQuest
Serials of Illinois Libraries Online (SILO)
South Carolina Public School Library Media Center Demonstration Project
South Dakota Library Network (SDLN)
Vermont Automated Library System (VALS)
Wisconsin Statewide Database Program (WISCAT)

SCHOOL LIBRARIES WITHIN A LIBRARY COOPERATIVE OR SYSTEM
Central Minnesota Libraries Exchange (CMLE) Automation
Central Minnesota Libraries Exchange (CMLE) Retrospective Conversion Project
Northwest Union Catalog and Interlibrary Loan System (NUCILS)
OCLC LS/2 Automation System
Rolling Prairie Library System CLSI Network
SMILE (Southcentral Minnesota Inter-Library Exchange)/Educational Cooperative
Service Unit automation project
South Jersey Union Catalog and ILL System
Starved Rock Library System CLSI Network
SWAN (System Wide Automated Network)

SCHOOL LIBRARIES WITH PUBLIC LIBRARIES
(Does not include projects listed as "State level or statewide projects",
"School libraries within a library cooperative or system" or "School librar-
ies with other types of libraries", which may include public libraries among
their participants.)
Birmingham Cooperative Circulation System
Carmel's Public Library/School Libraries Shared Integrated Online System
Fairbanks North Star Borough School District CLSI Project
First City Libraries Network
Henrico County Public Schools/Public Library Network
Neuse Regional Library/Lenoir County Schools
Project INFORM

SCHOOL LIBRARIES WITH OTHER TYPES OF LIBRARIES
(Public libraries may or may not be included in these projects. Does not
include those projects indexed under "State Level or Statewide Projects"
and "School Libraries within a Library Cooperative or System".)
Capital City Libraries
EASYLINK; ODIN; BACL
LMN Cooperative Circulation System
North Country Library Cooperative Multi-type Database Activities .
Sitka Library Network

Southside Virginia Library Network

VALNET

SCHOOL DISTRICT PROGRAMS
Broome-Delaware-Tioga BOCES School Library System
Eastern Oregon School Libraries Network

SCHOOL BUILDING PROGRAMS
Seven Oaks Elementary School Building Network

SHARED ONLINE CATALOG
Broome-Delaware-Tioga BOCES School Library System
Capital City Libraries
Carmel's Public Library/School Libraries Shared Integrated Online System
Cumberland Trail Library system Automated Services
EASYLINK, ODIN, BACL
Fairbanks North Star Borough School District CLSI Project
First City Libraries Network
OCLC LS/2 Automation System
Project INFORM
Rolling Prairie Library System CLSI Network
Sitka Library Network
South Dakota Library Network
SWAN (System Wide Automated Network)
VALNET

SHARED CIRCULATION SYSTEM
Birmingham Cooperative Circulation System
Capital City Libraries
Carmel's Public Library/School Libraries Shared Integrated Online System
Cumberland Trail Library System Automation Services
Eastern Oregon School Libraries Network
Fairbanks North Star Borough School District CLSI Project
First City Libraries Network
Henrico County Public Schools/Public Library Network
LMN Cooperative Circulation System
OCLC LS/2 Automation System
Rolling Prairie Library System CLSI Network
Sitka Library Network
South Dakota Library Network
Starved Rock Library System CLSI Network
SWAN (System Wide Automated Network)
VALNET

CD-ROM CATALOGS
ACCESS PENNSYLVANIA
Broome-Delaware-Tioga BOCES School Library System
Eastern Oregon School Libraries Network

Iowa Locator
Neuse Regional Library/Lenoir County Schools
Northwest Union Catalog and Interlibrary Loan System (NUCILS)
reQuest
South Jersey Union Catalog and ILL System
Wisconsin Statewide Database Program (WISCAT)

DIAL ACCESS TO ONLINE CATALOGS
EASYLINK, ODIN, BACL
OCLC LS/2 Automation System
SMILE (Southcentral Minnesota Inter-Library Exchange)/Educational Cooperative
Service Unit automation project
South Dakota Library Network
Southside Virginia Library Network I
Starved Rock Library System CLSI Network
Vermont Automated Library System (VALS)

INTERLIBRARY LOAN TELECOMMUNICATION SYSTEM
(INCLUDES FACSIMILE)
ACCESS PENNSYLVANIA
Broome-Delaware-Tioga BOCES School Library System
Capital City Libraries
Central Minnesota Libraries Exchange (CMLE) Automation
Eastern Oregon School Libraries Network
EASYLINK, ODIN, BACL
First City Libraries Network
Georgia Online Database (GOLD)
Iowa Locator
Neuse Regional Library/Lenoir County Schools
North Country Library Cooperative Multi-type Database Activities (not yet in place)
Northwest Union Catalog and Interlibrary Loan System (NUCILS)
OCLC LS/2 Automation System
Rolling Prairie Library System CLSI Network
South Carolina Public School Library Media Center Demonstration
Sitka Library Network
South Dakota Library Network
South Jersey Union Catalog and ILL System
Southside Virginia Library Network II
Starved Rock Library System CLSI Network
SWAN (System Wide Automated Network)
VALNET
Vermont Automated Library System
Wisconsin Statewide Database Program

INVENTORY
Carmel's Public Library/School Libraries Shared Integrated Online System
Cumberland Trail Library System Automation Services
Henrico County Public Schools/Public Library Network

MICROFORM CATALOGS
Broome-Delaware-Tioga BOCES School Library System
North Country Library Cooperative Multi-type Database Activities
Sitka Library Network
Wisconsin Statewide Database Program

ONLINE DATABASE SEARCH SERVICES
LIN-TEL

UNION LIST OF SERIALS
Alabama Union List of Serials
Broome-Delaware-Tioga BOCES School Library System
Georgia Online Database (GOLD)
North Country Library Cooperative Multi-type Database Activities
Serials of Illinois Libraries Online (SILO)

BUILDING NETWORK
(Includes online catalog, word processing, electronic mail, grade book)
Seven Oaks Elementary School Building Network

INDEX TO AUTOMATED SYSTEMS

Ameritech (originally Dataphase)
Cumberland Trail Library System Automation Services

Autographics
Northwest Union Catalog and Interlibrary Loan System (NUCILS)
reQuest

Bibliofile
Henrico County Public Schools/Public Library Network

Brodart
ACCESS PENNSYLVANIA
Broome-Delaware-Tioga BOCES School Library System
Wisconsin Statewide Database Program

BRS
LIN-TEL

CLSI
Carmel's Public Library/School Libraries Shared Integrated Online System
Cooperative Circulation System
Fairbanks North Star Borough School District CLSI Project
LMN Cooperative Circulation System
Rolling Prairie Library System CLSI Network
Starved Rock Library System CLSI Network
SWAN (System Wide Automated Network)

The Computer Company
Henrico County Public Schools/Public Library Network

Compuserver
Northwest Union Catalog and Interlibrary Loan System

Dynix
Eastern Oregon School Libraries Network

GRC-LaserQuest
Eastern Oregon School Libraries Network
North Country Library Cooperative Multi-type Database Activities
SMILE (Southcentral Minnesota Inter-Library Exchange)/Educational Cooperative
Service Unit automation project

Library Corporation's Intelligent Catalog
Neuse Regional Library/Lenoir County Schools

Library Information Systems
Capital City Libraries
Sitka Library Network

Marcive
Eastern Oregon School Libraries Network

MITINET
Wisconsin Statewide Database Program

OCLC Group Access Capability
Georgia Online Database (GOLD)

OCLC LS/2
OCLC LS/2 Automation System

OCLC MICROCON
Carmel's Public Library/School Libraries Shared Integrated Online System

OCLC Online Catalog
Broome-Delaware-Tioga BOCES School Library System
Carmel's Public Library/School Libraries Shared Integrated Online System
Serials of Illinois Libraries Online (SILO)

OCLC (SOLINET)
Alabama Union List of Serials
S.C. Public School Library Media Center Demonstration Project

Pueblo Library System
Henrico County Public Schools/Public Library Network

UNISYS PALS
Central Minnesota Libraries Exchange (CMLE) Automation
SMILE (Southcentral Minnesota Inter-Library Exchange)/Educational Cooperative
Service Unit automation project
South Dakota Library Network

VTLS
Southside Virginia Library Network I

Western Library Network (WLN)
Capital City Libraries
Sitka Library Network